CAPRICORN
DECEMBER
2002

TOTAL HOROSCOPE

JOVE BOOKS, NEW YORK

The publishers regret that they cannot answer individual letters requesting personal horoscope information.

2002 TOTAL HOROSCOPE: CAPRICORN

PRINTING HISTORY
Jove edition / June 2001

The Penguin Putnam Inc. World Wide Web site address is
http://www.penguinputnam.com

ISBN: 0-515-13076-1

A JOVE BOOK®
Jove Books are published by The Berkley Publishing Group,
a division of Penguin Putnam Inc.,
375 Hudson Street, New York, New York 10014.
JOVE and the "J" design
are trademarks belonging to Penguin Putnam Inc.

PRINTED IN THE UNITED STATES OF AMERICA

10 9 8 7 6 5 4 3 2 1

CONTENTS

MESSAGE TO CAPRICORN 5
CAPRICORN SNEAK PREVIEW OF THE
   21st CENTURY 13
THE CUSP-BORN CAPRICORN 15
CAPRICORN RISING: YOUR ASCENDANT 18
LOVE AND RELATIONSHIPS........................ 22
CAPRICORN: YOU AND YOUR MATE 25
CAPRICORN: YOUR PROGRESSED SUN 41
CAPRICORN BIRTHDAYS 44
CAN ASTROLOGY PREDICT THE FUTURE?...... 45
YOUR PLACE AMONG THE STARS................ 48
FREE CHOICE AND VALUE OF PREDICTIONS... 53
YOUR HOROSCOPE AND THE ZODIAC 58
THE SIGNS OF THE ZODIAC........................ 61
   The Signs and Their Key Words..................... 74
   The Elements and Qualities of the Signs 75
   The Planets and the Signs They Rule................ 80
   The Zodiac and the Human Body.................... 81
THE ZODIACAL HOUSES AND
   THE RISING SIGN............................... 82
THE PLANETS OF THE SOLAR SYSTEM 88
THE MOON IN ALL SIGNS.......................... 97
MOON TABLES 105
   Moon Sign Dates: 2002............................. 106
   Fishing Guide and Planting Guide: 2002............. 110
   Moon Phases: 2002................................. 111
LUCKY NUMBERS FOR CAPRICORN: 2002........ 112
CAPRICORN YEARLY FORECAST: 2002 113
CAPRICORN DAILY FORECAST: 2002 118
   July–December 2001 233

MESSAGE TO CAPRICORN

Dear Capricorn,

Capricorn is depth. You gain strength not from rushing from one job to the next, but from staying with a problem until it is solved. When you are jumpy, anxious, and unsettled, you need structure in your life, something to focus on and to which you can devote your efforts. Although you are secretly a dreamer, the major aim in your life is to deepen yourself in a given area, whatever you have chosen. If you are career-oriented, you move forward slowly, gaining experience, power, and position, always digging deeper into your work, learning, experiencing, climbing carefully, slipping here and there but never falling. You may lose ground, encounter setbacks, but each obstacle makes you more aware of the steps ahead.

You rarely feel you have already made it. You don't boast that you've arrived, because you are aware of how much farther you have to go. It is the slow, sure climb to the top that you are involved in, not simply the flash and pomp of enjoying the crown.

Capricorns may have experienced sudden reversals and changes in career status, professional upheavals, scandals, and anxieties, and unexpected events through their partners or other people. Many Capricorns have changed goals suddenly, left jobs, and no longer feel career or success-oriented at all. Actually, Capricorns try to remain relatively unchanged by upheavals. You like to feel impervious to bombardment from strange or alien forces. You are reluctant to have existing rules and patterns broken—rules and patterns that give your life endurance, safety, and stability. But when the upheaval and shouting is over, Capricorn may return to a safer, narrower point of view and enjoy the fruits of expanded experience and new visions of life. The development of the personal self will be achieved through that word mentioned earlier: depth.

If you are a homemaker, you're probably the greatest shopper to stalk the supermarket. If you're a movie star, you're ageless and irreplaceable. If you're a philosopher or scientist, you go to the heart of every question that arises. If you're into money, your mind is a busy cash register. You're an eager executive, smooth politician, ruthless dictator. You always affect the Establishment in some way. You are corruptible in your love of control. Otherwise you are generous, philosophical, talented, and wise. Whatever you do, if you're a Capricorn and happy, you do it well.

You'll often run into Capricorns who really don't achieve much or feel satisfaction or pride in the things they do. They are sloppy, irrational, and overemotional. Yes, overemotional! Capricorns often disapprove so strongly of being deep and sensible, they will live their lives being unreasonable, irresponsible, and careless. They are actually trying to find a balance between what they have been told all their lives they should be, and what they feel they should become. So they go on a reckless binge and later turn into sober, serious, sometimes cynical people. You may know people who do this who aren't Capricorns. But a deeper analysis of their horoscopes will show the influence of Capricorn in their lives.

You may feel that you have to be too serious and too responsible. Nobody likes to feel like a robot or a machine. Often you must throw off the burdens and sober frame of reference of your daily life and have a wild fling, an adventure just for the fun of it, to let yourself know there's a world out there with interesting things to see and learn. You won't be happy until you find a balance between your emotional self and your mental self. Often you'll attract people because of your stability and responsibility. You think at first they're going to mother you and take care of you. After a while you find yourself guarding and taking care of them. If they become too loving or motherly, you may reject them as weak or lazy. You can't resist the fruitful, artistic side of people, while at the same time you criticize an artistic way of life as unrespectable or unpredictable. This is one of your conflicts.

You crave security and emotional sustenance in a relationship, yet you often find it difficult to accept unlimited love, affection, and feeling from another human being. While you are soothed and bathed by the warmth another can bring you, many times you feel inhibited or prohibited from accepting it, for one practical reason or another. Whatever the reason, you believe that structure is necessary to life. You must define your emotional life in terms of limits, in the way the size and shape of a swimming pool will determine the exact amount of water it will hold.

If you know yourself well and recognize your needs, if you meet your emotions honestly and don't fear being inundated by them, you can find a loving, affectionate partner for a long-lasting, happy, successful relationship. If you are reluctant to look deep within yourself, the results can be disastrous. You are fiercely loyal and will blind your eyes to many of your partner's shortcomings when it comes to defending him or her against the outside world. You can be like a fort full of soldiers protecting the women and children inside from attack. Internally, though, things could be terribly different. You often hold things in and don't let anything inside get out and be free. When you are emotionally frightened, you close up. The reaction is chaos, coldness, separation, and the demise of what could be a beautiful marriage. It's a dilemma. If you could give yourself up totally to your emotions, without any thought of being reasonable, you'd end up having to work harder than before. Then you would have practical reasons to turn off romance.

In no way does this mean you lack the capacity to love someone. It simply signifies another aspect to love between two people. Love for the Capricorn is faith, devotion, loyalty, steadfastness, duty, reality, and deep underlying responsibility. If you pretend not to have a brain, the results will be so chaotic that you will eventually find it necessary to retreat into coldness, diffidence, and icy distance.

You can be an iceberg, to be sure. You are calculating, shrewd, stiff, unforgiving. You are manipulative and pragmatic and will use others when necessary. You often lack true sympathy, especially when you feel you are being invaded. There's a social climber in you with a stingy, disagreeable bitterness that can make you a dry, uncompromising rightwinger. You can use your tremendous capacity for organization and skillful diplomacy with people as a tool for the acquisition of power. You can sometimes enjoy controlling people and situations to the exclusion of genuine human feeling. When it suits you, you can turn off emotions and find undeniable reasons for doing so.

But the quality about you as a Capricorn that everyone needs in order to make a success out of anything—love or career—is the depth of understanding and patience that makes you what you are. If you will only give yourself over to developing it, you will be a master of understanding. What you lack in luster and fire, you make up for in profundity.

During the part of the year when the Sun is in the sign of Capricorn, Earth comes closest to the Sun. But the North Pole tips away from the Sun, so that we in the northern part of the globe are tipped away from the light. Thus nights are longer. Life slows down. The sap stays in the trees, the animals are hushed in their nests and caves with all the necessary food stored up for long nights ahead. Winter begins here, and there is a patient wait for the Earth to begin to tip toward the Sun again. There is no depression or hopelessness in the trees or animals. Something deep within them knows that spring will come this year as it does every year.

Capricorns do have the patience and endurance to wait for what they want. Their successes are often long in coming, but they do come, sure as springtime. But you often meet Capricorns who are hopeless and depressed, dark and gloomy, who dwell on trouble and sorrow. They seem to have replaced patience with despair. They have thrown out determination and live in narrow-minded poverty of the spirit.

You are Capricorn because you enjoy a certain comfort in aligning your aims and ambitions with the restrictions that prevent success, and then achieving success despite those restrictions. You lose valuable time when you dwell on the obstacle instead of the power within you to grow and succeed under the shadow of that obstacle. Your least attractive qualities are your downhearted tendency, which can discourage and deter people from their dreams, and your cynical yet controlling tendency to stand in someone's way. Your contribution is the helpful and loving understanding you can provide in pointing out certain inescapable facts, and then the way you go about removing any obstacles that might impede progress.

It is quite true that your life has responsibilities and burdens that others' may not have. But you choose a way of living that is most comfortable for you. You will ultimately feel best in accepting the role of responsible authoritarian, because in that way you can exercise your unbeatable qualities for problem solving.

If you are too conscious of your limitations and lack the confidence to carry out your goals, what is the source of your discouragement? Often you may have had a difficult childhood and may have lived with conditions and situations that impeded you from realizing your goals. There may have been poverty, or sickness, or problems in the environment that could not be erased, always bringing you down and keeping you from doing what you wanted to do. You may have had a parent who was critical or disapproving or even absent and not there to support you in your endeavors. There could be a problem of social condition, reputation, or prestige that caused you pain, embarrassment, or depression. Whatever the reason, you as a Capricorn must use that very limitation as the building block to your success as a mature adult.

You're often old when you're young, and then you grow into your skin as time goes on. As a child, if you weren't weak or sickly, there was probably a quality of the older person in you. The influence of elderly people and Father Time seems to be connected quite directly with Capricorn. Your skin may wrinkle early, or your hair may turn gray. But as time goes on, your well-conserved youth will begin to blossom long after the Sun has set for many of your contemporaries. If you worry too much about what may happen in the future, you miss all the fun of the present. If you are too worried about getting old, you never experience the heady carelessness of being young. What seems to be over-seriousness and overconcern with practicality in your youth will be the fruits of maturity in later years.

In one sense you're a born professional, with a capacity for self-discipline that will keep you in shape all the way to the top. Your teeth, bones, skin, knees, and joints are your major health areas with their reflex results on head, stomach, kidneys, and lower back. Good diet, hard work, and exercise are your tools to remaining healthy. Your occasional binges are necessary since so much of the time you try not to allow yourself indulgences and naughty luxuries. People wouldn't believe it from talking to you, but you are really quite indulgent, with a stronger taste for all kinds of pleasures than you allow yourself to admit.

You're surprisingly charitable about money. You often feel disappointment or confusion when dealing with brothers and sisters. You are ever striving to free yourself from parental or childhood programing. You're a great pleasure lover and you enjoy lavish good times, although you can't stop worrying about the expense, even if it isn't yours. In work you are bright, quick-minded, and easy to get along with on a superficial level. Although you are often restless, flighty, and easily bored, you conquer this boredom through persistence, determination, and concentration. When you devote yourself to a problem you are profound, thorough, imaginative, talented, and original. You can attack it from all angles at once so that the problem doesn't have a chance against your searching deliberate action. You're economical and thrifty, sometimes too stingy and callous, but with a natural dislike of waste and a mistrust of exaggeration.

The future frightens you because you fear the adoption of beliefs or codes of ethics that will undermine either your importance or your sense of values—both of which have been structured according to social conformity. Your strength and staying power are almost unmatchable. While many others would have surrendered long ago, you're just getting started. The hotter it gets around you, the cooler you become.

Sexually you can be a lot warmer than anyone would imagine. You could be bold, dashing, and astonishingly ardent. You can be an exotic, glamorous lover, sometimes too much concerned with the image you are making, but able to handle your powerful passions and desires. Like everything else, when you decide to do it, you've got to be the best.

You're always striving to perfect and purify your understanding of yourself and the world in general. Your code of conduct, although strictly pragmatic, is aiming at honesty, helpfulness, and sincere self-improvement. Your highest aims, strangely enough, often are not involved with career or profession. Your highest success often comes in the area of marriage. It gives you the feeling of greatest accomplishment.

You don't often show it immediately, but you are vastly more sensitive than you dare let on, and this can turn you inward. Then you set up outside defenses while you examine and reexamine your inside self.

In a way, you are like a well-constructed pyramid: perfect and architecturally correct, mysteriously implacable, very hard to know. You are organized to a high degree, have been built to last and last and last. You are practical and useful, yet magnificently dignified, signifying permanence and finality and reflecting careful planning from the beginning.

Like the pyramid, laid stone by stone, you are successful only after great effort. When you get to the top, you can be pretty narrow. Yet you are the eternal riddle of beauty, the paradox of the ages, complete with properties no one will ever know.

Michael Lutin

CAPRICORN SNEAK PREVIEW
OF THE 21st CENTURY

As the decade opens on a new century, indeed on a new millennium, the planets set the stage for change and challenge. Themes connecting present and future are in play. Already planetary influences that emerged from the century just past are showing the drama unfolding in the twenty-first century. These influences reveal hidden paths and personal hints for achieving your potential—your message from the planets.

Capricorn individuals, ruled by wise planet Saturn, are experiencing great activity and profound change. A major shift in your life is coming from Pluto in Sagittarius. Pluto in Sagittarius into year 2008 urges you to confront basic truths. The past must be put into perspective so you can reach your potential.

With Pluto in fiery Sagittarius you delve deep into your unconcious, tap into your private reserves of imagination and wisdom, let dreams lead you on a path of self-discovery. Although the journey may be painful at times, the rewards can be liberating if you summon the courage to participate fully.

Key to the journey is Saturn, your ruling planet, as it guides you in the twenty-first century. Saturn in Taurus till April 2001 highlights money, status, and love of the beautiful. But Capricorn caution weighs against daredevil risks, chancy schemes, and cheap thrills. Saturn in Taurus provides richness and depth on which to build elegant structures.

Saturn in Gemini till early June 2003 invites participation in the lively world of idea and thought. The rooted wisdom of Saturn steadies the sparkling intellect of mercurial Gemini. With Saturn in Gemini you communicate a penetrating analysis while letting your capricious side show.

Saturn in Cancer to mid-July 2005 unlocks doors to inner life. New challenges await in the emotional realm. Saturn in Cancer makes you work on the feeling side of things. This cycle resonates for Capricorn because Cancer is your zodiacal partner as well as your zodiacal opposite. Saturn in Cancer indicates dynamism, conflict, resolution. Fruitful alliances can be forged.

Influences from good-luck planet Jupiter are in sync with your planet Saturn. Jupiter in Gemini to July 2001 speeds development of new ideas and projects. Promote while negotiating skills are at peak. Jupiter in Cancer to early August 2002 starts a potentially profitable cycle, again because Cancer is your zodiacal partner. Ties combining love and business are fortunate. You may marry into money.

Jupiter in Leo to late August 2003 ushers in self-expression and expansion. This cycle opposes the saturnine tendency toward restriction. Yet the outward pull of Jupiter in Leo overcomes hesitating shyness since the planets Uranus and Neptune are in outgoing Aquarius, a sign kin to yours because it is co-ruled by your planet Saturn.

Uranus and Neptune cycles complement the expansive trend of Pluto in Sagittarius and Jupiter in Leo. Uranus, planet of innovation, is in Aquarius into year 2003. Uranus in Aquarius helps you let go of old constraints. It gives freedom to express emotion long pent up. Neptune, planet of visionary thought, is in Aquarius into year 2012. Neptune in Aquarius removes inhibitions to grow the intellectual and spiritual sides of your life. With Saturn as your guide, travel and spread ideas, choose golden opportunities, realize long-cherished dreams.

THE CUSP-BORN CAPRICORN

Are you *really* a Capricorn? If your birthday falls around Christmas, at the very beginning of Capricorn, will you still retain the traits of Sagittarius, the sign of the Zodiac before Capricorn? What if you were born during the 3rd week of January—are you more Aquarius than Capricorn? Many people born at the edge, or cusp, of a sign have great difficulty determining exactly what sign they are. If you are one of these people, here's how you can figure it out, once and for all.

Consult the table on page 17. Find the year of your birth, and then note the day. The table will tell you the precise days on which the Sun entered and left your sign. Whether you were born at the beginning or end of Capricorn, yours is a lifetime reflecting a process of subtle transformation. Your life on Earth will symbolize a significant change in consciousness, for you are either about to enter a whole new way of living, or you are leaving one behind.

If you were born at the beginning of Capricorn, you may want to read the horoscope book for Sagittarius as well as Capricorn, for Sagittarius is a deep—often hidden—part of your spirit. You were born with the special gift of being able to bring your dreams into reality and put your talents and ambitions to practical use.

You need to conquer worry and depression and learn to take life seriously, but without losing your sense of humor and hope. You must find a balance between believing nothing and believing too much. You need to find the firm middle ground between cynicism and idealism.

If you were born at the end of Capricorn, you may want to read the horoscope book on Aquarius, for you are a dynamic mixture of both the Capricorn and Aquarius natures.

You are in a transitional state of consciousness, about to enter a whole new way of living, but still dutybound to perform responsibilities before you are set free. You are bound by two lifestyles, one conservative, the other freedom-oriented. You combine the talents of regularity and discipline with rebellious spontaneity and flashing genius.

You can be troubled by reversals and setbacks, despite your serious planning, and find great conflict between personal ambitions and deep desires for freedom. You have a great pull toward the future, but you are powerfully drawn back to society and cultural conditioning.

THE CUSPS OF CAPRICORN

DATES SUN ENTERS CAPRICORN
(LEAVES SAGITTARIUS)

December 22 every year from 1900 to 2010,
except for the following:

December 21

1912	1952	1972	1988	2000
16	53	73	89	2001
20	56	76	92	2002
23	57	77	93	2004
28	60	80	94	2005
32	61	81	96	2006
36	64	84	97	2008
40	65	85	98	2009
44	68	86		2010
48	69			

DATES SUN LEAVES CAPRICORN
(ENTERS AQUARIUS)

January 20 every year from 1900 to 2010,
except for the following:

January 19			January 21		
1977	1989	2001	1903	1920	1932
81	93	2005	04	24	36
85	97	2009	08	28	44
			12		

CAPRICORN RISING:
YOUR ASCENDANT

Could you be a "double" Capricorn? That is, could you have Capricorn as your Rising sign as well as your Sun sign? The tables on pages 20–21 will tell you Capricorns what your Rising sign happens to be. Just find the hour of your birth, then find the day of your birth, and you will see which sign of the Zodiac is your Ascendant, as the Rising sign is called. For a detailed discussion on how the Rising sign is determined, see pages 82–85.

Your Ascendant, or Rising sign, modifies your basic Sun sign personality, and it affects the way you act out the daily predictions for your Sun sign. If your Rising sign is indeed Capricorn, what follows is a description of its effects on your horoscope. If your Rising sign is some other sign of the Zodiac, you may wish to read the horoscope book for that sign.

With Capricorn Rising, look to beautiful planet Saturn, your ruler. Saturn makes you philosophical and wise, with a penchant for lone pursuits. You can see reality from many perspectives. And you are motivated to test the viability of each framework you discover. But you want to test life your own way, and be accountable only to yourself. Planet Saturn gives you a melancholy turn of mind.

You have an immense respect for the best order of things, for the way people should relate to each other in order to support each other. And you want to weave this order and support into the fabric of your own life and also into the larger tapestry of society as a whole. Your underlying drive is to integrate concepts of how people should behave with your self-concept. You start with a principle, then you expand it.

You have a remarkable ability to create far-reaching plans and to see them through. You can put kaleidoscopic images into focus. You can galvanize scattered energies into a powerful momentum. You are an excellent manager of people. You are happiest when you have unlimited responsibility to carry out such tasks. A family or a company is grist for your mill. Power to you means the ability to achieve your aims. Power is not fame, fortune, fondness, or any other measure of how people judge you. You are your own judge.

Capricorn Rising individuals are sensitive to the ways people treat your principles. In your mind your identity and your principles are merged. So when your ideas are insulted, you are insulted. You dislike rule breakers, and for that you may earn a reputation for sternness. You detest traitors, philanderers, cheats of all kinds. And for that you may be called rigid and old-fashioned. You consider a breach of trust and a lack of support dishonorable, because such behavior is harmful and hurtful. And you can be pitiless in your scorn for the perpetrator.

Your persona may be so identified with your principles that you restrain your impulses and suppress your emotions. You may refuse to let joy show even though you are probably the first one to see the humor in a situation. You will try to make your feelings fit your preconceptions instead of letting feelings build ideas. It is hard for you to tolerate contradiction and ambiguity. Only when emotion and idea match, can you relax and go with the flow.

The key words for Capricorn Rising are form and focus. Your own uphill struggle is a model of success for those who would despair and give in. Don't conserve your talents in seclusion. Connect on deep levels and help people build their lives.

RISING SIGNS FOR CAPRICORN

Hour of Birth	Day of Birth		
	December 21–26	December 27–31	January 1–5
Midnight	Virgo; Libra 12/22	Libra	Libra
1 AM	Libra	Libra	Libra
2 AM	Libra	Libra; Scorpio 12/29	Scorpio
3 AM	Scorpio	Scorpio	Scorpio
4 AM	Scorpio	Scorpio	Scorpio; Sagittarius 1/5
5 AM	Sagittarius	Sagittarius	Sagittarius
6 AM	Sagittarius	Sagittarius	Sagittarius
7 AM	Sagittarius	Capricorn	Capricorn
8 AM	Capricorn	Capricorn	Capricorn
9 AM	Capricorn; Aquarius 12/26	Aquarius	Aquarius
10 AM	Aquarius	Aquarius	Aquarius; Pisces 1/2
11 AM	Pisces	Pisces	Pisces
Noon	Pisces; Aries 12/22	Aries	Aries
1 PM	Aries; Taurus 12/26	Taurus	Taurus
2 PM	Taurus	Taurus	Gemini
3 PM	Gemini	Gemini	Gemini
4 PM	Gemini	Gemini	Cancer
5 PM	Cancer	Cancer	Cancer
6 PM	Cancer	Cancer	Cancer
7 PM	Cancer; Leo 12/22	Leo	Leo
8 PM	Leo	Leo	Leo
9 PM	Leo	Leo; Virgo 12/30	Virgo
10 PM	Virgo	Virgo	Virgo
11 PM	Virgo	Virgo	Virgo

	Day of Birth		
Hour of Birth	**January 6–10**	**January 11–15**	**January 16–21**
Midnight	Libra	Libra	Libra
1 AM	Libra	Libra; Scorpio 1/13	Libra
2 AM	Scorpio	Scorpio	Scorpio
3 AM	Scorpio	Scorpio	Scorpio; Sagittarius 1/21
4 AM	Sagittarius	Sagittarius	Sagittarius
5 AM	Sagittarius	Sagittarius	Sagittarius
6 AM	Sagittarius; Capricorn 1/7	Capricorn	Capricorn
7 AM	Capricorn	Capricorn	Capricorn
8 AM	Capricorn; Aquarius 1/7	Aquarius	Aquarius
9 AM	Aquarius	Aquarius	Aquarius; Pisces 1/17
10 AM	Pisces	Pisces	Pisces; Aries 1/21
11 AM	Aries	Aries	Aries
Noon	Aries; Taurus 1/10	Taurus	Taurus
1 PM	Taurus	Taurus; Gemini 1/15	Gemini
2 PM	Gemini	Gemini	Gemini
3 PM	Gemini	Gemini; Cancer 1/15	Cancer
4 PM	Cancer	Cancer	Cancer
5 PM	Cancer	Cancer	Cancer; Leo 1/21
6 PM	Leo	Leo	Leo
7 PM	Leo	Leo	Leo
8 PM	Leo	Leo; Virgo 1/14	Virgo
9 PM	Virgo	Virgo	Virgo
10 PM	Virgo	Virgo	Virgo; Libra 1/21
11 PM	Libra	Libra	Libra

LOVE AND RELATIONSHIPS

No matter who you are, what you do in life, or where your planets are positioned, you still need to be loved, and to feel love for other human beings. Human relationships are founded on many things: infatuation, passion, sex, guilt, friendship, and a variety of other complex motivations, frequently called love.

Relationships often start out full of hope and joy, the participants sure of themselves and sure of each other's love, and then end up more like a pair of gladiators than lovers. When we are disillusioned, bitter, and wounded, we tend to blame the other person for difficulties that were actually present long before we ever met. Without seeing clearly into our own natures we will be quite likely to repeat our mistakes the next time love comes our way.

Enter Astrology.

It is not always easy to accept, but knowledge of ourselves can improve our chances for personal happiness. It is not just by predicting when some loving person will walk into our lives, but by helping us come to grips with our failures and reinforce our successes.

Astrology won't solve all our problems. The escapist will ultimately have to come to terms with the real world around him. The hard-bitten materialist will eventually acknowledge the eternal rhythms of the infinite beyond which he can see or hear. Astrology does not merely explain away emotion. It helps us unify the head with the heart so that we can become whole individuals. It helps us define what it is we are searching for, so we can recognize it when we find it.

Major planetary cycles have been changing people's ideas about love and commitment, marriage, partnerships, and relationships. These cycles have affected virtually everyone in areas of personal involvement. Planetary forces point out upheavals and transformations occurring in all of society. The concept of marriage is being totally reexamined. Exactly what the changes will ultimately bring no one can tell. It is usually difficult to determine which direction society will take. One thing is certain: no man is an island. If the rituals and pomp of wedding ceremonies must be revised, then it will happen.

Social rules are being revised. Old outworn institutions are indeed crumbling. But relationships will not die. People are putting less stress on permanence and false feelings of security. The emphasis now shifts toward the union of two loving souls. Honesty, equality, and mutual cooperation are the goals in modern marriage. When these begin to break down, the marriage is in jeopardy. Surely there must be a balance between selfish separatism and prematurely giving up.

There is no doubt that astrology can establish the degree of compatibility between two human beings. Two people can share a common horizon in life but have quite different habits or basic interests. Two others might have many basic characteristics in common while needing to approach their goals from vastly dissimilar points of view. Astrology describes compatibility based on these assumptions.

It compares and contrasts through the fundamental characteristics that draw two people together. Although they could be at odds on many basic levels, two people could find themselves drawn together again and again. Sometimes it seems that we keep being attracted to the same type of individuals. We might ask ourselves if we have learned anything from our past mistakes. The answer is that there are qualities in people that we require and thus seek out time and time again. To solve that mystery in ourselves is to solve much of the dilemma of love, and so to help ourselves determine if we are approaching a wholesome situation or a potentially destructive one.

We are living in a very curious age with respect to marriage and relationships. We can easily observe the shifting social attitudes concerning the whole institution of marriage. People are seeking everywhere for answers to their own inner needs. In truth, all astrological combinations can achieve compatibility. But many relationships seem doomed before they get off the ground. Astrologically there can be too great a difference between the goals, aspirations, and personal outlook of the people involved. Analysis of both horoscopes must and will indicate enough major planetary factors to keep the two individuals together. Call it what you will: determination, patience, understanding, love—whatever it may be, two people have the capacity to achieve a state of fulfillment together. We all have different needs and desires. When it comes to choosing a mate, you really have to know yourself. If you know the truth about what you are really looking for, it will make it easier to find. Astrology is a useful, almost essential, tool to that end.

In the next chapter your basic compatibility with each of the twelve signs of the Zodiac is generalized. The planetary vibrations between you and an individual born under any given zodiacal sign suggest much about how you will relate to each other. Hints are provided about love and romance, sex and marriage so that you and your mate can get the most out of the relationship that occupies so important a role in your life.

CAPRICORN:
YOU AND YOUR MATE

CAPRICORN—ARIES

Aries creativity, zest, and super confidence can make a brilliant combination with Capricorn patience, method, and determination. Aries has the driving force and Capricorn has the way with people. Together you can accomplish the impossible. Of course, Aries will think it takes too long and Capricorn will think it's a little harebrained or crazy. But when you put your heads together to confer or conspire, the result is the successful execution of any Herculean task.

Tension will be great in such a relationship, since the fire of the Aries spirit must submit to the cool, earthy approach of Capricorn stability and practicality. The worried Capricorn's need for control will be upset by Aries' stubborn independence and refusal to knuckle under to facts. But understanding and a mutual desire for growth can prevent a frustrating stalemate, a deadlock that even time cannot solve.

You can weather professional battles, crisis situations, and romantic storms for the purpose of sharing your goals. You both need sustenance and security. Any burdens or responsibilities that circumstances impose on your lives can help you grow closer and more determined to succeed through loving each other.

Hints for Your Aries Mate

This alliance combines the Aries spontaneity of youthful aggression and the Capricorn caution of seasoned determination. Both of you want to get somewhere important. In the beginning you'll help each other and take advantage of your differences to score points against people and situations who would hold you back. As your relationship continues, you might have difficulty holding on to each other, as your very differences may be seen as holding each other back, too. You will automatically check your bank balance when Aries suggests new expenditures, and Aries is likely to suggest some wild and foolish ones. Aries will resent you for appearing skeptical. Try to be as charming with your Aries mate when you are alone together, doing your mutual bookkeeping, as you are in public, where your debonair attitude smooths the feathers Aries has ruffled. You need each other.

CAPRICORN—TAURUS

To thaw out a Capricorn, bring a Taurus around and watch the results. Slowly the ice melts and gradually the temperature rises. This is a blend that grows more compatible with time. You are both stubborn, cautious, and resistant to external change or control. But you look upon life in much the same way. Once you've established yourselves with the confidence of your own individual beings, you are warm and appreciative of one another.

Where your union may lack wild excitement, you provide depth of understanding, loyalty, and steadfast devotion. Where the two of you have been wild, uncontrollably passionate, or irresponsible, you will begin to feel maturity, security, and responsible faithfulness. Money and status will play a significant role in your union. Your position in the community will be crucial at some meaningful moment in your choices and decisions. You are the union of the need for luxury and the spartan capacity to sacrifice.

Together you can be the symbols of greed, ambition,

and lust to get ahead. You can be the picture of narrowness and fearful, penny-pinching gloom. But through love and cooperation, you can be the reflection of success through perseverence, determination, and your love for the beautiful things in life.

Hints for Your Taurus Mate

Here is one relationship where you don't have to be afraid to show your feelings. Your Taurus mate has the most wondrous way of making things feel all right, even when you are convinced the world is against you. Taurus does this naturally. But unless your mate begins to see some tangible rewards for his or her magic touch, he or she will just as magically wander off to more appreciative arms. And the rewards you bestow don't have to be all material ones. In fact, Taurus may suspect that you suspect he or she is a golddigger if you consistently show praise through things. Inspire the artist in your mate; after all, Taurus has some lovely natural talents which sometimes go unnoticed because they are not being used to make a living. Inspire your Taurus to sing, sew, dance, design, paint, potter; but be sure the effort is not connected with homemaking, or your mate will feel you're taking advantage. The best inspiration, of course, is lovemaking on all levels of expression.

CAPRICORN—GEMINI

If you want to make this relationship work, you will have to come to terms with the conflicts in your own nature. And if you have been drawn to Gemini, there are some mighty strong riddles to be solved. You have formed a strange union that pits depth and seriousness against restless curiosity—the need for security and stability against eternal craving for change. This may seem such a fundamental conflict that you give up and end the relationship before giving it a chance. But the conflict is within each of you.

You both require regularity, order, and discipline. But you both also have an equivocal, ambiguous streak that rejects the sober, thrifty, wise course of action in favor of reckless, trial-and-error superficiality. You both need the certainty of a life constructed out of honest hard work, method, and determination. At the same time, each of you is repelled by a plodding everyday life and cannot survive without versatility, mobility, and change.

In order to make anything lasting out of this relationship, you and your partner need to recognize the conflicts within yourselves, before solving the riddle of your relationship.

Hints for Your Gemini Mate

In this alliance, you and your Gemini mate will always be involved in high-powered situations because your Gemini mate thinks that way. The simplest thing can become an epic. Notwithstanding her or his logic, Gemini loves complications. You, who like to pursue the fabrics of life one thread at a time until they are raveled neatly or woven straightly, will be constantly startled and probably upset. Calm down. Gemini will never get you in trouble, and besides you'll never have a dull moment. If you do try to conserve your mate's talents for the unexpected or the bizarre, you will end up repressing them and her or him as well. That pall could spell the end of the affair. So be more tolerant, more alive to your Gemini lover's special way of loving you, of bringing you morsels of life into the livingroom to admire and engage. Get engaged; share your lover's dictum that variety is the spice of life.

CAPRICORN—CANCER

This is one of the best combinations in the whole Zodiac. You join emotional intimacy with worldly strength, the strong union of home life and business success. Provided you can accept your roles maturely, you have one of the strongest ties going. The natural process of long-term change will teach both of you a great deal about the potentials and pitfalls of such a combination.

Problems in your relationship usually occur when one of you plays the starving baby—insecure, misunderstood, and neglected. The other one plays the cold, unresponsive stepparent, the implacable and unyielding head of the orphanage. Such a Capricorn-Cancer relationship soon reaches a crisis stage—you either split up or grow up. Then when you assume your adult roles, accepting each other and yourselves, you can set about living your happy lives.

At worst, you can be uptight, status-seeking conformists, repressing every drive but the drive to get ahead. You can both be caught in a war between feelings of rejection and a cold, gloomy fear of love.

At best, you can encourage each other to succeed, and can grow more fully in the knowledge and security of each other's love. To respect each other's need for silence, introspection, and separateness is to accept each other's need for communion, fulfillment, and completion. The key is to transform yourselves into healthy adults, uniting the faculties of head and heart, feeling and reason.

Hints for Your Cancer Mate

Your natural reserves of patience and your natural reticence will get a good working out in this relationship with moody Cancer. Although you respect privacy, wanting it a great deal for yourself as well, you may begin to think that your Cancer mate carries his or her preoccupation with it to an extreme. Sometimes you will get the feeling that Cancer believes the world revolves around him or her alone. It won't do you any good to batter down the emotional gates, Goat that you are. Your Cancer lover's unyielding exterior is a resistant barrier. Yet do not be fooled into thinking your mate is not sensitive. Quite the contrary is true, and you can be the perfect lover if you keep that fact number one in your mind and number one in your behavior. While your mate is having a sulk, tend to the joint responsibilities of your union; don't let things go adrift. Cancer will want to come back to that cozy, loving nest.

CAPRICORN—LEO

At first you might think this is an unlikely combination, like moving a tropical island to the North Pole. But you two have many things in common, and can bring each other to greater growth, development, and maturity. You'll complain about Leo's constant demands—emotional and practical—and you'll meet problems that will be insurmountable to younger or immature members of your respective zodiacal signs.

You are both strong people who like to be in control of your lives. You dislike feeling that you're hardening, getting old or rusty or unattractive. You both like to feel in command of your emotions and are both concerned with the image (or spectacle) you're making of yourself. You're both ambitious, conservative animals imbued with the drive, determination, and stamina to get what you want.

When you don't get your own way, you both can get ugly. Yet you are both honorable, constant, and desirous of doing your best and being great at whatever you do. Capricorn makes Leo work and points out all the unfinished tasks that must be done in order for Leo to make it in the world. Leo turns Capricorn on, financially, professionally, or sexually, and the pair can do a lot together. This relationship reflects your need to unify the hot with the cold within yourself, to temper the passion of youth with the responsibility of a mature parent figure.

Hints for Your Leo Mate

Together you share one quality in common with your Leo mate that could either be a boon to the relationship or make it a bust. That is your unfailing honesty about calling things the way you see them. Both of you insist on telling the other things that might make another person blush or bolt. But fortunately both of you only do this in private; both you and Leo hate public scenes and would rather die than embarrass each other in front of other people. This candor, which you two have developed in the context of a loving relationship, is quite unusual. If you can keep it from causing friction with each other, your relationship will work. But sometimes neither one of you appreciates the bluntness or brutality. Now develop your basic charming way into a soothing facade for your Leo mate on those occasions when she or he feels really down, discouraged, ego-hurt. Leo needs pampering. Surely that won't discredit your honesty or wear out your endurance.

CAPRICORN—VIRGO

You are a truly harmonious pair. You may be critical of each other, but you can depend on each other for sound advice. However, don't make the mistake of invading each other's privacy or taking undue liberties.

You can develop your capacity to love and understand both yourselves and each other by the steady steps of trusting, helping, and being reasonable. Virgo loves with a deep, sincere affection that flows slowly with time, a solid emotion of steadfast, secure love. You will each know your responsibilities to each other and your loyalties will be called upon as long as your relationship lasts. You are both earnest, shy creatures, repelled by your own practicality, but able to accept each other because you feel so many of the same things.

Capricorn and Virgo together can be fearful of emotion. At worst, your fears make you petty and small, criticizing and disapproving, but cloaking your disdain in polite conversation. You can be narrow and prejudiced. Neither of you can bear being controlled by others, although you often feel you are, and you may not always express your fears candidly. You could talk a lot and not say what you feel. In time, no matter what, your love deepens and your trust grows.

But you can be honestly affectionate with each other, if a little distant. Virgo's presence in your life can offer invaluable help in philosophy, work, and career. Clarity of vision is your mutual strong point.

Hints for Your Virgo Mate

Perhaps no one can appreciate your solemn, saturnine qualities better than your Virgo mate. She or he will be able to read much humor and irony in what others may take only for a seasoned wisdom, dry of emotion and devoid of wit. That's why you are drawn to Virgo; Virgo truly appreciates the rich, varied underside of your emotional life, which few people get a chance to see, let alone experience. Don't treat your Virgo lover merely as the admiring critic, the aloof onlooker. Get in there and make Virgo experience his or her own deep underside, as well as vicariously enjoying yours. Here is someone shyer than you, more finicky than you, possibly even afraid. You have brain and brawn, so put them in the service of making your Virgo lover secure and ready to take a risk on serious lovemaking. The fringe benefits will be a wild abandon, a carefree excursion into mind and body both of you might not dare without the other.

CAPRICORN—LIBRA

Capricorn and Libra together form a serious combination of loyalty and stability. You provide each other with the homey security and driving ambition for career that both require. Either of you may be rebuffed and feel emotionally cheated at times, for the warmth that you feel you deserve is not always what you really need. But you're quite a pair—loyal, sturdy, and perfectly matched. Conservative and somewhat old-fashioned, you are status-conscious and often slightly insecure about your position.

The Capricorn-Libra combination can symbolize the union of beauty and practicality, and your home reflects it. When one of you is unresponsive, the other one goes crazy. When one of you is dreamy and unrealistic, there's trouble at home. Don't get caught in someone else's arms either. That's real trouble for the relationship.

In a relationship with Libra there will be great changes in the way you both approach business and social life. There will be transformations in both your personas, too. You are both more sharply aware of your ambitions and needs, as individuals and together. What keeps your relationship alive is a union of tact and determination. Of all the Capricorn pairings around the Zodiac, Capricorn-Libra can see each other through crises as nobody can.

Hints for Your Libra Mate

Being attractive to yourself, to your mate, and to other people who see you in a relationship is one of the great benefits of having a Libra lover. You will never doubt your attractiveness. Your native charm and way with people will get a big boost from Libra, who likes to show you off in company. You'll never have more friends, fanciers, hangers-on. You might get tired of it, feel a little boxed in, and begin to withdraw from Libra's gay world of sparkle, glitter, and glib conversation. That negative response could get you right out of the relationship, and you only intended to put a curfew on party time. So try, gallantly, to go along with the lovely social ideas of your Libra, even if you can't truly enjoy them. On the positive side, you can do much more. Build a big, broad base of success and wisdom from which your Libra mate can operate, and always be there to settle the controversies. Love is your main mutual asset.

CAPRICORN—SCORPIO

If you have developed a relationship based on mutual respect, you can be a source of strength to each other. You can be truly good friends—maybe better friends than lovers. Yours is a conflict between intensity and stability. At best you can be a turned-on couple with one eye open to reality. Sexually, this can be a powerful match, for the involvement is anything but light. You share a need for strong ties, and the depth of your involvement will always show that.

On the other hand, games of power and control are irresistible, for you both have strong wills and must feel that you are indispensable to your partner. You need acceptance, and must be loved, honored, and obeyed. When you go to war, your weapons will be totally different, and the war could last long on both sides. Neither of you is a total forgiver and forgetter.

Through loyalty and practicality your relationship is sure to deepen no matter how long it takes. And it will take time, for you are both hard to know. You are both able, courageous people and no struggle is too great for you to undertake. The older you get the tougher you get. Maturity brings new wisdom to your association.

You are a very powerful combination of sex and career drive, though sometimes you are more successful apart than you are together.

Hints for Your Scorpio Mate

You will certainly be regarded as an authority figure in this relationship, whether you are one or not. Your Scorpio mate may feel all bets are off. He or she may not even try to convince you, gall you, trick you, maneuver you. Temper, tantrum, tumult will be the name of the game; tactics have gone out the window. Well, at least you won't have to cope with your lover's slyness or sting; you'll have your hands full managing all the emotion. Maybe, though, that's the wrong way to respond to your Scorpio lover. Managing is not exactly what they want. They turn to you for the real response, the unguarded one, the spontaneous one. To you, it may seem a childish one, because all your life the unguarded response was the one you felt most likely to fail. That belief is probably the karma between you and Scorpio. If you are long on patience, you can get your lover out of their childishness and into your world. If you can't, no amount of good sex will keep you together.

CAPRICORN—SAGITTARIUS

If you get this act together in time, you'll be a smash hit on the planet Earth. The enthusiasm and casual resilience of Sagittarius combines well with the thoughtful planning and determined ambition of Capricorn. You bring Sagittarius down to earth when it comes to money. When you begin to build a financial reality out of your very real practical needs, your secret belief in luck starts paying off tangibly. Sagittarius, although often your undoing, broadens your scope and makes a fuller life possible.

At worst, your lives together may suffer from lack

of realism, depth, and determination and a painful inconsistency. You may bounce from a casual and careless ease to a greedy search for concrete stability and security, from a stubborn decision to flout facts and enjoy yourself to the grim awakening of life's ironies.

But at best, you and Sagittarius together are the union of dreams and concrete reality. You can together embody wisdom, learning, and a true enrichment of mutual experience. You know how to enjoy yourselves and still face the responsibilities of your adult lives.

Hints for Your Sagittarius Mate

Sometimes in this relationship you will get the feeling that your Sagittarius mate sweet-talked you into something. You're never quite sure what it is. If you go about the business of the relationship sternly, trying to organize the vague threads of emotional and economic commitment into a tight fabric of living, you'll be less sure as time goes on. Sagittarius probably did sweet-talk you because she or he liked you. That does not mean in any way that Sagittarius can be like you. Forget that identity of wills, of purpose right away. The only identity you two can have is in bed, and don't sell that short. You'll be much happier having your romantic sweetheart where it counts. Go on about the business of life by yourself. Don't push Sagittarius into your mode. On the positive side, try to be ultratolerant of your mate's meanderings and irresponsibilities. Sexual love and intellectual respect are what you two can have together.

CAPRICORN—CAPRICORN

You are a modest and socially reserved couple. You are the masters of diplomacy and protocol, dutiful and considerate, polite and restrained. You are the prototypes of good breeding, no matter what your origins.

Your affection for each other will be genuine, no matter what sort of relationship you are involved in. You respect each other's privacy and can help each other in your careers or in dealing with some major obstacle that keeps you from achieving your ends.

Your relationship will grow into fruitfulness through a shared responsibility or burden, a circumstance that you both can use to build happy, useful lives.

You should be on your guard against gloom and neurotic fear. Avoid miserliness and cynicism, for you could use them to freeze each other out.

Though you are not wildly demonstrative, your understated devotion to each other is inspiring to others. Your love is deep, sincere, honest—built upon unshakable foundations of loyalty and trust. You understand each other's struggles in a total way.

Hints for Your Capricorn Mate

You two are probably secretly celebrating your togetherness, complimenting each other on having chosen so wisely, yet wondering all the while what other astrological configurations exist in your individual makeups that make you seem so different from one another. Who ever said that Capricorn is a one-dimensional creature? Besides, your curiosity together is probably the glue that cements you. You both could have a grand and satisfying time with each other, coming home at the end of the day to share your trials and tribulations, without need of company. Yet beware! That set between you could become so rigid you both lose your feel for real life if it is not reflected between the two of you. Which one of you will change first and abandon the other? Change together. Build a room onto your house every year, not just to look out of but to invite other people into. In that way, you'll have a lot more to mirror back and forth without abandoning each other.

CAPRICORN—AQUARIUS

You're an interesting pair because you can be very close while still being so deeply different. Together both of you feel the need to be shy and reserved, and yet long to be explosively spontaneous. Neither of you enjoys being bombed out of your reserved self, but you don't like your desires curtailed by any controlling forces.

Capricorn and Aquarius together can be torn between rigid discipline and chaotic disruption, caught by conflicts between your ambitions and your sense of independence. Each of you must accept and respect the other's need for privacy, independence, and security.

For this relationship to develop properly, you must give your Aquarius freedom and ask for support in return. You both desire liberation from life's limiting routines, and method is your greatest tool to that end. The relationship is complex, to say the least.

At best, you and Aquarius are the union of reason and genius, the symbol of the orderly transition from the old to the new.

Hints for Your Aquarius Mate

In this relationship you are reminded to rely on the planet that you and your Aquarius mate share: Saturn. Chances are you two got together in the first place because in that crowded room of crazy people each of you recognized a kindred soul—each other. Your gift for organizing information and Aquarius' gift for circulating information exchanged. Zip—you got together. You both may still do that, and it eases your relationship enormously. But every now and then you get the feeling that if you had been seeing more clearly, you would have seen your Aquarius also to be a little crazy. How come your lover is so unpredictable yet gloomy, so flagrant yet afraid, so scattered yet certain?

In the large view of things, obviously Uranus, the co-ruling planet of Aquarius, is messing things up. So bring the big gun, the planet Saturn, to the rescue. Show your Aquarius how to overcome the contradictions in personality. But let him or her show you the radical side of lovemaking and sexual excitement.

CAPRICORN—PISCES

Both Capricorn and Pisces combine hardheaded pragmatism and idle dreaminess. Each of you has that individual riddle to solve, and must come to terms with yourself if you are to be happy together.

Basically, you are a harmonious pair, happy in silent company, coming together and parting. You need to respect the tides of your separate lives, for together you are like high seas crashing against the rocks in passionate thunder, leaving again when the tide goes out.

Your conflict is between concrete facts and vague abstract theories, between reason and emotion, the belief that life is made up of hard and tough realities that must be faced and the passive belief that everything is illusion and nothing really matters. The greatest danger to your relationship is that you will become involved in a silent, agonizing war between everyday reality and wishful poetry. It is important to develop the capacity to accept within yourselves the strange phobias and conflicts between head and heart that are part of both of you.

Together you can find a balance between believing nothing and believing too much. Once you learn to avoid fearful separatism and melting together in weak dependency, you add deep dimensions to each other's lives, through the totality of emotional contact and through the counsel of reason.

Hints for Your Pisces Mate

Hard cane sugar is what you and your Pisces lover can crop if you're sensible about it. Don't let that moon-light-and-molasses look fool you. Pisces is not all that sultry, and certainly not that lazy. Pisces is not dew, but the sea. And there's always a cold, biting chop to an ocean current riding on top of the waves. So it is with your relationship. Don't waste a lot of time trying to get your Pisces mate in line. And don't insult or mock their particular form of discipline. Do your own thing. But keep attuned for that special sound—a dim, rhythmic echo of earth pounding on earth by waves. Your own sound maybe? If you want structure, go back to the fields and harvest cane sugar together. If you want freedom, listen to your Pisces mate's dreams— don't scoff—and go where earth can regenerate. Your union is essentially sexual and melodramatic, so make the most of it.

CAPRICORN:
YOUR PROGRESSED SUN

WHAT IS YOUR NEW SIGN?

Your birth sign, or Sun sign, is the central core of your whole personality. It symbolizes everything you try to do and be. It is your main streak, your major source of power, vitality, and life. But as you live you learn, and as you learn you progress. The element in your horoscope that measures your progress is called the Progressed Sun. It is the symbol of your growth on Earth, and represents new threads that run through your life. The Progressed Sun measures big changes, turning points, and major decisions. It will often describe the path you are taking toward the fulfillment of your desires.

Below you will find brief descriptions of the Progressed Sun in three signs. According to the table on page 43, find out about your Progressed Sun and see how and where you fit into the cosmic scheme. Each period lasts about 30 years, so watch and see how dramatic these changes turn out to be.

If Your Sun Is Progressing Into—

AQUARIUS, you'll be wanting freedom from the restrictions of the past years. You will want to break new territory, throw off limitations, start fresh, and experiment with new things and new people. You will have contact with groups, societies, and friends. This is a time for advancement and putting past reversals into perspective.

PISCES, a spiritual need for reconciling failure with success is necessary. Guilt, disappointment, and sorrow are illusions that must be pierced, for beyond them lies redemption. If you are plagued by doubts, anxieties, or uncertainties, be assured that success and happiness will come through devotion, faith, compassion, forgiveness, and love.

ARIES, you start gathering a sense of who you are and a basic zest and enthusiasm for life. You speak up for yourself and become more open and honest. You'll feel more aggressive and will respond to challenges more readily. You may even look for challenge. You are experiencing an awakening of self.

HOW TO USE THE TABLE

Look for your birthday in the table on the facing page. Then, under the appropriate column, find out approximately when your Progressed Sun will lead you to a new sign. From that point on, for 30 years, the thread of your life will run through that sign. Read the definitions on the preceding pages and see exactly how that life thread will develop.

For example, if your birthday is December 31, your Progressed Sun will enter Aquarius around your 21st birthday and will travel through Aquarius until you are 51 years old. Your Progressed Sun will then move into Pisces. Reading the definitions of Aquarius and Pisces will tell you much about your major involvements and interests during those years.

YOUR PROGRESSED SUN

If your birthday falls on:	start looking at AQUARIUS at age	start looking at PISCES at age	start looking at ARIES at age
Dec. 22	30	60	90
23	29	59	89
24	28	58	88
25	27	57	87
26	26	56	86
27	25	55	85
38	24	54	84
29	23	53	83
30	22	52	82
31	21	51	81
January 1	20	50	80
2	19	49	79
3	18	48	78
4	17	47	77
5	16	46	76
6	15	45	75
7	14	44	74
8	13	43	73
9	12	42	72
10	11	41	71
11	10	40	70
12	9	39	69
13	8	38	68
14	7	37	67
15	6	36	66
16	5	35	65
17	4	34	64
18	3	33	63
19	2	32	62
20	1	31	61

CAPRICORN BIRTHDAYS

Dec. 21	Chris Evert, Jane Fonda
Dec. 22	E. A. Robinson, Lady Bird Johnson
Dec. 23	Jose Greco
Dec. 24	Howard Hughes, Ava Gardner
Dec. 25	Clara Barton, Little Richard
Dec. 26	Mao, Steve Allen
Dec. 27	Marlene Dietrich, Pasteur
Dec. 28	Woodrow Wilson, Maggie Smith
Dec. 29	Pablo Casals, Mary Tyler Moore
Dec. 30	Kipling, Bo Diddley
Dec. 31	Henri Matisse, Odetta
Jan. 1	Betsy Ross, Herbert Hoover, Xavier Cugat
Jan. 2	Stalin, Isaac Asimov, Renata Tebaldi
Jan. 3	Lucretia Mott, Zasu Pitts, Ray Milland
Jan. 4	Newton, Jacob Grimm
Jan. 5	Konrad Adenauer, Yogananda
Jan. 6	St. Joan, Tom Mix, Alan Watts
Jan. 7	Charles Addams, Emma Nevada
Jan. 8	Elvis Presley, Frances Workman
Jan. 9	Nixon, Gypsy Rose Lee, Joan Baez
Jan. 10	Ray Bolger, Galina Ulanova
Jan. 11	Eva le Gallienne, William James
Jan. 12	Vivekananda, Joe Frazier, Texas Guinan
Jan. 13	Horatio Alger
Jan. 14	Albert Schweitzer, Faye Dunaway
Jan. 15	Onassis, Nasser, Margaret O'Brien
Jan. 16	Ethel Merman, Eartha Kitt
Jan. 17	Ben Franklin, Al Capone
Jan. 18	Cezanne, Janis Joplin, Poe, Robert E. Lee
Jan. 19	Desi Arnaz, George Burns
Jan. 20	Federico Fellini, Pat Neal

CAN ASTROLOGY PREDICT THE FUTURE?

Can astrology really peer into the future? By studying the planets and the stars is it possible to look years ahead and make predictions for our lives? How can we draw the line between ignorant superstition and cosmic mystery? We live in a very civilized world, to be sure. We consider ourselves modern, enlightened individuals. Yet few of us can resist the temptation to take a peek at the future when we think it's possible. Why? What is the basis of such universal curiosity?

The answer is simple. Astrology works, and you don't have to be a magician to find that out. We certainly can't prove astrology simply by taking a look at the astonishing number of people who believe in it, but such figures do make us wonder what lies behind such widespread popularity. Everywhere in the world hundreds of thousands of serious, intelligent people are charting, studying, and interpreting the positions of the planets and stars every day. Every facet of the media dispenses daily astrological bulletins to millions of curious seekers. In Eastern countries, the source of many wisdoms handed down to us from antiquity, astrology still has a vital place. Why? Surrounded as we are by sophisticated scientific method, how does astrology, with all its bizarre symbolism and mysterious meaning, survive so magnificently? The answer remains the same. It works.

Nobody knows exactly where astrological knowledge came from. We have references to it dating back to the dawn of human history. Wherever there was a stirring of human consciousness, people began to observe the natural cycles and rhythms that sustained their life. The diversity of human behavior must have been evident even to the first students of consciousness. Yet the basic similarity between members of the human family must have led to the search for some common source, some greater point of origin somehow linked to the heavenly bodies ruling our sense of life and time. The ancient world of Mesopotamia, Chaldea, and Egypt was a highly developed center of astronomical observation and astrological interpretation of heavenly phenomena and their resultant effects on human life.

Amid the seeming chaos of a mysterious unknown universe, people from earliest times sought to classify, define, and organize the world around them. Order: that's what the human mind has always striven to maintain in an unceasing battle with its natural counterpart, chaos, or entropy. We build cities, countries, and empires, subjugating nature to a point of near defeat, and then ... civilization collapses, empires fall, and cities crumble. Nature reclaims the wilderness. Shelly's poem *Ozymandias* is a hymn to the battle between order and chaos. The narrator tells us about a statue, broken, shattered, and half-sunk somewhere in the middle of a distant desert. The inscription reads: "Look on my works, ye mighty, and despair." And then we are told: "Nothing beside remains. Round the decay of that colossal wreck, boundless and bare, the lone and level sands stretch far away."

People always feared the entropy that seemed to lurk in nature. So we found permanence and constancy in the regular movements of the Sun, Moon, and planets and in the positions of the stars. Traditions sprang up from observations of the seasons and crops. Relationships were noted between phenomena in nature and the configurations of the heavenly bodies. This "synchronicity," as it was later called by Carl Jung, extended to thought, mood, and behavior, and as such developed the astrological archetypes handed down to us today.

Astrology, a regal science of the stars in the old days, was made available to the king, who was informed of impending events in the heavens, translated of course to their earthly meanings by trusted astrologers. True, astrological knowledge in its infant stages was rudimentary and beset with many superstitions and false premises. But those same dangers exist today in any investigation of occult or mystical subjects. In the East, reverence for astrology is part of religion. Astrologer-astronomers have held respected positions in government and have taken part in advisory councils on many momentous issues. The duties of the court astrologer, whose office was one of the most important in the land, were clearly defined, as early records show.

Here in our sleek Western world, astrology glimmers on, perhaps more brilliantly than ever. With all of our technological wonders and complex urbanized environments, we look to astrology even now to cut through artificiality, dehumanization, and all the materialism of contemporary life, while we gather precious information that helps us live in that material world. Astrology helps us restore balance and get in step with our own rhythms and the rhythms of nature.

Intelligent investigation of astrology (or the practical application of it) need not mean blind acceptance. We only need to see it working, see our own lives confirming its principles every day, in order to accept and understand it more. To understand ourselves is to know ourselves and to know all. This book can help you to do that—to understand yourself and through understanding develop your own resources and potentials as a rich human being.

YOUR PLACE AMONG THE STARS

Humanity finds itself at the center of a vast personal universe that extends infinitely outward in all directions. In that sense each is a kind of star radiating, as our Sun does, to all bodies everywhere. These vibrations, whether loving, helpful, or destructive, extend outward and generate a kind of "atmosphere" in which woman and man move. The way we relate to everything around us—our joy or our sorrow—becomes a living part of us. Our loved ones and our enemies become the objects of our projected radiations, for better or worse. Our bodies and faces reflect thoughts and emotions much the way light from the Sun reflects the massive reactions occurring deep within its interior. This energy and light reach all who enter its sphere of influence.

Our own personal radiations are just as potent in their own way, really. The reactions that go on deep within us profoundly affect our way of thinking and acting. Our feelings of joy or satisfaction, frustration or anger, must eventually find an outlet. Otherwise we experience the psychological or physiological repercussions of repression. If we can't have a good cry, tell someone our troubles, or express love, we soon feel very bad indeed.

As far as our physical selves are concerned, there is a direct relationship between our outer lives, inner reactions and actions, and the effects on our physical body. We all know the feeling of being startled by the sudden ring of a telephone, or the simple frustration of missing a bus. In fact, our minds and bodies are constantly reacting to outside forces. At the same time we, too, are generating actions that will cause a reaction in someone else. You may suddenly decide to phone a friend. If you are a bus driver you might speed along on your way and leave behind an angry would-be passenger. Whatever the case, mind and body are in close communication and they both reflect each other's condition. Next time you're really angry take a good long look in the mirror!

In terms of human evolution, our ability to understand, control, and ultimately change ourselves will naturally affect all of our outside relationships. Astrology is invaluable to helping us comprehend our inner selves. It is a useful tool in helping us retain our integrity, while cooperating with and living in a world full of other human beings.

Let's go back to our original question: Can astrology predict the future? To know that, we must come to an understanding of what the future is.

In simplest terms the future is the natural next step to the present, just as the present is a natural progression from the past. Although our minds can move from one to the other, there is a thread of continuity between past, present, and future that joins them together in a coherent sequence. If you are reading this book at this moment, it is the result of a real conscious choice you made in the recent past. That is, you chose to find out what was on these pages, picked up the book, and opened it. Because of this choice you may know yourself better in the future. It's as simple as that.

Knowing ourselves is the key to being able to predict and understand our own future. To learn from past experiences, choices, and actions is to fully grasp the present. Coming to grips with the present is to be master of the future.

"Know thyself" is a motto that takes us back to the philosophers of ancient Greece. Mystery religions and cults of initiation throughout the ancient world, schools of mystical discipline, yoga and mental expansion have always been guardians of this one sacred phrase. Know thyself. Of course, that's easy to say. But how do you go about it when there are so many conflicts in our lives and different parts of our personalities? How do we know when we are really "being ourselves" and not merely being influenced by the things we read or see on television, or by the people around us? How can we differentiate the various parts of our character and still remain whole?

There are many methods of classifying human beings into types. Body shapes, muscular types, blood types, and genetic types are only a few. Psychology has its own ways of classifying human beings according to their behavior. Anthropology studies human evolution as the body-mind response to environment. Biology watches physical development and adaptations in body structure. These fields provide valuable information about human beings and the ways they survive, grow, and change in their search for their place in eternity. Yet these branches of science have been separate and fragmented. Their contribution has been to provide theories and data, yes, but no lasting solutions to the human problems that have existed since the first two creatures realized they had two separate identities.

It's often difficult to classify yourself according to these different schemes. It's not easy to be objective about yourself. Some things are hard to face; others are hard to see. The different perspectives afforded to us by studying the human organism from all these different disciplines may seem contradictory when they are all really trying to integrate humankind into the whole of the cosmic scheme.

Astrology can help these disciplines unite to seek a broader and deeper approach to universal human issues. Astrology's point of view is vast. It transcends racial, ethnic, genetic, environmental, and even historical criteria, yet somehow includes them all. Astrology embraces the totality of human experience, then sets about to examine the relationships that are created within that experience.

We don't simply say, "The planets cause this or that." Rather than merely isolating cause or effect, astrology has unified the ideas of cause and effect. Concepts of past, present, and future merge and become, as we shall see a little later on, like stepping-stones across the great stream of mind. Observations of people and the environment have developed the astrological principles of planetary "influence," but it must be remembered that if there is actual influence, it is mutual. As the planets influence us, so we influence them, for we are forever joined to all past and future motion of the heavenly bodies. This is the foundation of astrology as it has been built up over the centuries.

ORDER VS. CHAOS

But is it all written in the stars? Is it destined that empires should thrive and flourish, kings reign, lovers love, and then ... decay, ruin, and natural disintegration hold sway? Have we anything to do with determining the cycles of order and chaos? The art of the true astrologer depends on his ability to uncover new information, place it upon the grid of data already collected, and then interpret what he sees as accurate probability in human existence. There may be a paradox here. If we can predict that birds will fly south, could we not, with enough time and samples for observation, determine their ultimate fate when they arrive in the south?

The paradox is that there is no paradox at all. Order and chaos exist together simultaneously in one observable universe. At some remote point in time and space the Earth was formed, and for one reason or another, life appeared here. Whether the appearance of life on planets is a usual phenomenon or an unrepeated accident we can only speculate at this moment. But our Earth and all living things upon its surface conform to certain laws of physical materiality that our observations have led us to write down and contemplate. All creatures, from the one-celled ameba to a man hurrying home at rush hour, have some basic traits in common. Life in its organization goes from the simple to the complex with a perfection and order that is both awesome and inspiring. If there were no order to our physical world, an apple could turn into a worm and cows could be butterflies.

But the world is an integrated whole, unified with every other part of creation. When nature does take an unexpected turn, we call that a mutation. This is the exciting card in the program of living experience that tells us not everything is written at all. Spontaneity is real. Change is real. Freedom from the expected norm is real. We have seen in nature that only those mutations that can adapt to changes in their environment and continue reproducing themselves will survive. But possibilities are open for sudden transformation, and that keeps the whole world growing.

FREE CHOICE AND
THE VALUE OF PREDICTIONS

Now it's time to turn our attention to the matter of predictions. That was our original question after all: Can astrology peer into the future? Well, astrological prognostication is an awe-inspiring art and requires deep philosophical consideration before it is to be undertaken. Not only are there many grids that must be laid one upon the other before such predictions can be made, but there are ethical issues that plague every student of the stars. How much can you really see? How much should you tell? What is the difference between revealing valuable data and disclosing negative or harmful programing?

If an astrologer tells you only the good things, you'll have little confidence in the analysis when you are passing through crisis. On the other hand, if the astrologer is a prophet of doom who can see nothing but the dark clouds on the horizon, you will eventually have to reject astrology because you will come to associate it with the bad luck in your life.

Astrology itself is beyond any practitioner's capacity to grasp it all. Unrealistic utopianism or gloomy determinism reflect not the truth of astrology but the truth of the astrologer interpreting what he sees. In order to solve problems and make accurate predictions, you have to be *able* to look on the dark side of things without dwelling there. You have to be able to take a look at all the possibilities, all the possible meanings of a certain planetary influence without jumping to premature conclusions. Objective scanning and assessment take much practice and great skill.

No matter how skilled the astrologer is, he cannot assume the responsibility for your life. Only you can take that responsibility as your life unfolds. In a way, the predictions of this book are glancing ahead up the road, much the way a road map can indicate turns up ahead this way or that. You, however, are still driving the car.

What, then, is a horoscope? If it is a picture of you at your moment of birth, are you then frozen forever in time and space, unable to budge or deviate from the harsh, unyielding declarations of the stars? Not at all.

The universe is always in motion. Each moment follows the moment before it. As the present is the result of all past choices and action, so the future is the result of today's choices. But if we can go to a planetary calendar and see where planets will be located two years from now, then how can individual free choice exist? This is a question that has haunted authors and philosophers since the first thinkers recorded their thoughts. In the end, of course, we must all reason things out for ourselves and come to our own conclusions. It is easy to be impressed or influenced by people who seem to know a lot more than we do, but in reality we must all find codes of beliefs with which we are the most comfortable.

But if we can stretch our imaginations up, up above the line of time as it exists from one point to another, we can almost see past, present, and future, all together. We can almost feel this vibrant thread of creative free choice that pushes forward at every moment, actually causing the future to happen! Free will, that force that changes the entire course of a stream, exists within the stream of mind itself—the collective mind, or intelligence, of humanity. Past, present, and future are mere stepping-stones across that great current.

Our lives continue a thread of an intelligent mind

that existed before we were born and will exist after we die. It is like an endless relay race. At birth we pick up a torch and carry it, lighting the way with that miraculous light of consciousness of immortality. Then we pass it on to others when we die. What we call the *unconscious* may be part of this great stream of mind, which learns and shares experiences with everything that has ever lived or will ever live on this world or any other.

Yet we all come to Earth with different family circumstances, backgrounds, and characteristics. We all come to life with different planetary configurations. Indeed each person *is* different, yet we are all the same. We have different tasks or responsibilities or lifestyles, but underneath we share a common current—the powerful stream of human intelligence. Each of us has different sets of circumstances to deal with because of the choices he or she has made in the past. We all possess different assets and have different resources to fall back on, weaknesses to strengthen, and sides of our nature to transform. We are all what we are now because of what we were before. The present is the sum of the past. And we will be what we will be in the future because of what we are now.

It is foolish to pretend that there are no specific boundaries or limitations to any of our particular lives. Family background, racial, cultural, or religious indoctrinations, physical characteristics, these are all inescapable facts of our being that must be incorporated and accepted into our maturing mind. But each person possesses the capacity for breakthrough, forgiveness, and total transformation. It has taken millions of years since people first began to walk upright. We cannot expect an overnight evolution to take place. There are many things about our personalities that are very much like our parents. Sometimes that thought makes us uncomfortable, but it's true.

It's also true that we are not our parents. You are

you, just you, and nobody else but you. That's one of the wondrous aspects of astrology. The levels on which each planetary configuration works out will vary from individual to individual. Often an aspect of selfishness will be manifested in one person, yet in another it may appear as sacrifice and kindness.

Development is inevitable in human consciousness. But the direction of that development is not. As plants will bend toward the light as they grow, so there is the possibility for the human mind to grow toward the light of integrity and truth. The Age of Aquarius that everyone is talking about must first take place within each human's mind and heart. An era of peace, freedom, and community cannot be legislated by any government, no matter how liberal. It has to be a spontaneous flow of human spirit and fellowship. It will be a magnificent dawning on the globe of consciousness that reflects the joy of the human heart to be part of the great stream of intelligence and love. It must be generated by an enlightened, realistic humanity. There's no law that can put it into effect, no magic potion to drink that will make it all come true. It will be the result of all people's efforts to assume their personal and social responsibilities and to carve out a new destiny for humankind.

As you read the predictions in this book, bear in mind that they have been calculated by means of planetary positions for whole groups of people. Thus their value lies in your ability to coordinate what you read with the nature of your life's circumstances at the present time. You have seen how many complex relationships must be analyzed in individual horoscopes before sensible accurate conclusions can be drawn. No matter what the indications, a person has his or her own life, own intelligence, basic native strength that must ultimately be the source of action and purpose. When you are living truthfully and in harmony with what you know is right, there are no forces, threats, or obstacles that can defeat you.

With these predictions, read the overall pattern and see how rhythms begin to emerge. They are not caused by remote alien forces, millions of miles out in space. You and the planets are one. What you do, they do. What they do, you do. But can you change their course? No, but you cannot change many of your basic characteristics either. Still, within that already existing framework, you are the master. You can still differentiate between what is right for you and what is not. You can seize opportunities and act on them, you can create beauty and seek love.

The purpose of looking ahead is not to scare yourself. Look ahead to enlarge your perspective, enhance your overall view of the life *you* are developing. Difficult periods cause stress certainly, but at the same time they give you the chance to reassess your condition, restate and redefine exactly what is important to you, so you can cherish your life more. Joyous periods should be lived to the fullest with the happiness and exuberance that each person richly deserves.

YOUR HOROSCOPE AND THE
ZODIAC

It's possible that in your own body, as you read this passage, there exist atoms as old as time itself. You could well be the proud possessor of some carbon and hydrogen (two necessary elements in the development of life) that came into being in the heart of a star billions and billions of years ago. That star could have exploded and cast its matter far into space. This matter could have formed another star, and then another, until finally our Sun was born. From the Sun's nuclear reactions came the material that later formed the planets—and maybe some of that primeval carbon or hydrogen. That material could have become part of the Earth, part of an early ocean, even early life. These same atoms could well have been carried down to the present day, to this very moment as you read this book. It's really quite possible. You can see how everything is linked to everything else. Our Earth now exists in a gigantic universe that showers it constantly with rays and invisible particles. You are the point into which all these energies and influences have been focused. You are the prism through which all the light of outer space is being refracted. You are literally a reflection of all the planets and stars.

Your horoscope is a picture of the sky at the moment of your birth. It's like a gigantic snapshot of the positions of the planets and stars, taken from Earth. Of course, the planets never stop moving around the Sun even for the briefest moment, and you represent that motion as it was occurring at the exact hour of your birth at the precise location on the Earth where you were born.

When an astrologer is going to read your chart, he or she asks you for the month, day, and year of your birth. She also needs the exact time and place. With this information he sets about consulting various charts and tables in his calculation of the specific positions of the Sun, Moon, and stars, relative to your birthplace when you came to Earth. Then he or she locates them by means of the *Zodiac*.

The Zodiac is a group of stars, centered against the Sun's apparent path around the Earth, and these star groups are divided into twelve equal segments, or *signs*. What we are actually dividing up is the Earth's path around the Sun. But from our point of view here on Earth, it seems as if the Sun is making a great circle around our planet in the sky, so we say it's the Sun's apparent path. This twelvefold division, the Zodiac, is like a mammoth address system for any body in the sky. At any given moment, the planets can all be located at a specific point along this path.

Now where are you in this system? First you look to your *Sun sign*—the section of the Zodiac that the Sun occupied when you were born. A great part of your character, in fact the central thread of your whole being, is described by your Sun sign. Each sign of the Zodiac has certain basic traits associated with it. Since the Sun remains in each sign for about thirty days, that divides the population into twelve major character types. Of course, not everybody born the same month will have the same character, but you'll be amazed at how many fundamental traits you share with your astrological cousins of the same birth sign, no matter how many environmental differences you boast.

The dates on which the Sun sign changes will vary from year to year. That is why some people born near the *cusp*, or edge, of a sign have difficulty determining their true birth sign without the aid of an astrologer who can plot precisely the Sun's apparent motion (the Earth's motion) for any given year. But to help you find your true Sun sign, a Table of Cusp Dates for the years 1900 to 2010 is provided for you on page 17.

Here are the twelve signs of the Zodiac as western astrology has recorded them. Listed also are the symbols associated with them and the *approximate* dates when the Sun enters and exits each sign for the year 2002.

Aries	Ram	March 20–April 20
Taurus	Bull	April 20–May 21
Gemini	Twins	May 21–June 21
Cancer	Crab	June 21–July 22
Leo	Lion	July 22–August 23
Virgo	Virgin	August 23–September 22
Libra	Scales	September 23–October 23
Scorpio	Scorpion	October 23–November 22
Sagittarius	Archer	November 22–December 21
Capricorn	Sea Goat	December 21–January 20
Aquarius	Water Bearer	January 20–February 18
Pisces	Fish	February 18–March 20

In a horoscope the *Rising sign*, or Ascendant, is often considered to be as important as the Sun sign. In a later chapter (see pages 82–84) the Rising sign is discussed in detail. But to help you determine your own Rising sign, a Table of Rising Signs is provided for you on pages 20–21.

THE SIGNS OF THE ZODIAC

The signs of the Zodiac are an ingenious and complex summary of human behavioral and physical types, handed down from generation to generation through the bodies of all people in their hereditary material and through their minds. On the following pages you will find brief descriptions of all twelve signs in their highest and most ideal expression.

ARIES
The Sign of the Ram

Aries is the first sign of the Zodiac, and marks the beginning of springtime and the birth of the year. In spring the Earth begins its ascent upward and tips its North Pole toward the Sun. During this time the life-giving force of the Sun streams toward Earth, bathing our planet with the kiss of warmth and life. Plants start growing. Life wakes up. No more waiting. No more patience. The message has come from the Sun: Time to live!

Aries is the sign of the Self and is the crusade for the right of an individual to live in unimpeachable freedom. It represents the supremacy of the human will over all obstacles, limitations, and threats. In Aries there is unlimited energy, optimism, and daring, for it is the pioneer in search of a new world. It is the story of success and renewal, championship, and victory. It is the living spirit of resilience and the power to be yourself, free from all restrictions and conditioning. There is no pattern you *have* to repeat, nobody's rule you *have* to follow.

Confidence and positive action are born in Aries, with little thought or fear of the past. Life is as magic as sunrise, with all the creative potential ahead of you for a new day. Activity, energy, and adventure characterize this sign. In this sector of the Zodiac there is amazing strength, forthrightness, honesty, and a stubborn refusal to accept defeat. The Aries nature is forgiving, persuasive, masterful, and decisive.

In short, Aries is the magic spark of life and being, the source of all initiative, courage, independence, and self-esteem.

TAURUS
The Sign of the Bull

Taurus is wealth. It is not just money, property, and the richness of material possessions, but also a wealth of the spirit. Taurus rules everything in the visible world we see, touch, hear, smell, taste—the Earth, sea, and sky—everything we normally consider "real." It is the sign of economy and reserve, for it is a mixture of thrift and luxury, generosity and practicality. It is a blend of the spiritual and material, for the fertility of the sign is unlimited, and in this sense it is the mystical bank of life. Yet it must hold the fruit of its efforts in its hands and seeks to realize its fantasy-rich imagination with tangible rewards.

Loyalty and endurance make this sign perhaps the most stable of all. We can lean on Taurus, count on it, and it makes our earthly lives comfortable, safe, pleasurable. It is warm, sensitive, loving, and capable of magnificent, joyful sensations. It is conservative and pragmatic, with a need to be sure of each step forward. It is the capacity to plan around eventualities without living in the future. Steadfast and constant, this is a sturdy combination of ruggedness and beauty, gentleness and unshakability of purpose. It is the point at which we join body and soul. Unselfish friend and loyal companion, Taurus is profoundly noble and openly humanitarian. Tenacity and concentration slow the energy down to bring certain long-lasting rewards.

Taurus is a fertile resource and rich ground to grow in, and we all need it for our ideas and plans to flourish. It is the uncut diamond, symbolizing rich, raw tastes and a deep need for satisfaction, refinement, and completion.

GEMINI
The Sign of the Twins

Gemini is the sign of mental brilliance. Communication is developed to a high degree of fluidity, rapidity, fluency. It is the chance for expressing ideas and relaying information from one place to another. Charming, debonair, and lighthearted, it is a symbol of universal interest and eternal curiosity. The mind is quick and advanced, with a lightning-like ability to assimilate data.

It is the successful manipulation of verbal or visual language and the capacity to meet all events with objectivity and intelligence. It is light, quick wit, with a comic satiric twist. Gemini is the sign of writing or speaking.

Gemini is the willingness to try anything once, a need to wander and explore, the quick shifting of moods and attitudes being a basic characteristic that indicates a need for change. Versatility is the remarkable Gemini attribute. It is the capacity to investigate, perform, and relate over great areas for short periods of time and thus to connect all areas. It is mastery of design and perception, the power to conceptualize and create by putting elements together—people, colors, patterns. It is the reporter's mind, plus a brilliant ability to see things in objective, colorful arrangement. Strength lies in constant refreshment of outlook and joyful participation in all aspects of life.

Gemini is involvement with neighbors, family and relatives, telephones, arteries of news and communication—anything that enhances the human capacity for communication and self-expression. It is active, positive, and energetic, with an insatiable hunger for human interchange. Through Gemini bright and dark sides of personality merge and the mind has wings. As it flies it reflects the light of a boundless shining intellect. It is the development of varied talents from recognition of the duality of self.

Gemini is geared toward enjoying life to the fullest by finding, above all else, a means of expressing the inner self to the outside world.

CANCER
The Sign of the Crab

Cancer is the special relationship to home and involvement with the family unit. Maintaining harmony in the domestic sphere or improving conditions there is a major characteristic in this sector of the Zodiac. Cancer is attachment between two beings vibrating in sympathy with one another.

It is the comfort of a loving embrace, a tender generosity. Cancer is the place of shelter whenever there are lost or hungry souls in the night. Through Cancer we are fed, protected, comforted, and soothed. When the coldness of the world threatens, Cancer is there with gentle understanding. It is protection and understated loyalty, a medium of rich, living feeling that is both psychic and mystical. Highly intuitive, Cancer has knowledge that other signs do not possess. It is the wisdom of the soul.

It prefers the quiet contentment of the home and hearth to the busy search for earthly success and civilized pleasures. Still, there is a respect for worldly knowledge. Celebration of life comes through food. The sign is the muted light of warmth, security, and gladness, and its presence means nourishment. It rules fertility and the instinct to populate and raise young. It is growth of the soul. It is the ebb and flow of all our tides of feeling, involvements, habits, and customs.

Through Cancer is reflected the inner condition of all human beings, and therein lies the seed of knowledge out of which the soul will grow.

LEO
The Sign of the Lion

Leo is love. It represents the warmth, strength, and regeneration we feel through love. It is the radiance of life-giving light and the center of all attention and activity. It is passion, romance, adventure, and games. Pleasure, amusement, fun, and entertainment are all part of Leo. Based on the capacity for creative feeling and the desire to express love, Leo is the premier sign. It represents the unlimited outpouring of all that is warm and positive.

It is loyalty, dignity, responsibility, and command. Pride and nobility belong to Leo, and the dashing image of the knight in shining armor, of the hero, is part of Leo. It is a sense of high honor and kingly generosity born out of deep, noble love. It is the excitement of the sportsman, with all the unbeatable flair and style of success. It is a strong, unyielding will and true sense of personal justice, a respect for human freedom, and an enlightened awareness of people's needs.

Leo is involvement in the Self's awareness of personal talents and the desire and need to express them. At best it is forthrightness, courage and efficiency, authority and dignity, showmanship, and a talent for organization. Dependable and ardent, the Lion is characterized by individuality, positivism, and integrity.

It is the embodiment of human maturity, the effective individual in society, a virile creative force able to take chances and win. It is the love of laughter and the joy of making others happy. Decisive and enthusiastic, the Lion is the creative producer of the Zodiac It is the potential to light the way for others.

♍

VIRGO
The Sign of the Virgin

Virgo is the sign of work and service. It is the symbol of the farmer at harvest time, and represents tireless efforts for the benefit of humanity, the joy of bringing the fruits of the Earth to the table of mankind. Celebration through work is the characteristic of this sign.

Sincerity, zeal, discipline, and devotion mark the sign of the Virgin.

The key word is purity, and in Virgo lies a potential for unlimited self-mastery. Virgo is the embodiment of perfected skill and refined talent. The thread of work is woven into the entire life of Virgo. All creativity is poured into streamlining a job, classifying a system, eradicating unnecessary elements of pure analysis. The true Virgo genius is found in separating the wheat from the chaff.

Spartan simplicity characterizes this sign, and Virgo battles the war between order and disorder. The need to arrange, assimilate, and categorize is great; it is the symbol of the diagnostician, the nurse, and the healer. Criticism and analysis describe this sign—pure, incisive wisdom and a shy appreciation of life's joys. All is devoted to the attainment of perfection and the ideal of self-mastery.

Virgo is the sign of health and represents the physical body as a functioning symbol of the mental and spiritual planes. It is the state of healing the ills of the human being with natural, temperate living. It is maturation of the ego as it passes from a self-centered phase to its awareness and devotion to humanity.

It is humanitarian, pragmatic, and scientific, with boundless curiosity. Focus and clarity of mind are the strong points, while strength of purpose and shy reserve underlie the whole sign. There is separateness, aloofness, and solitude for this beacon of the Zodiac. As a lighthouse guides ships, so Virgo shines.

LIBRA
The Sign of the Scales

Libra is the sign of human relationship, marriage, equality, and justice. It symbolizes the need of one human being for another, the capacity to find light, warmth, and life-giving love in relationship to another human being. It is union on any level—mental, sexual, emotional, or business. It is self-extension in a desire to find a partner with whom to share our joys. It is the capacity to recognize the needs of others and to develop to the fullest our powers of diplomacy, good taste, and refinement.

Libra is harmony, grace, aesthetic sensibility, and the personification of the spirit of companionship. It represents the skill to maintain balances and the ability to share mutually all life's benefits, trials, crises, and blessings. Libra is mastery at anticipation of another's needs or reactions. It is the exercise of simple justice with impartial delicacy.

It is the need to relate, to find a major person, place, or thing to sustain us and draw out our attention. It is growth through becoming awakened to the outside world and other people. It is the union of two loving souls in honesty, equality, mutual cooperation, and mutual accord.

SCORPIO
The Sign of the Scorpion

Scorpio is the sign of dark intensity, swirling passion, and sexual magnetism. It is the thirst for survival and regeneration that are the bases of sexual orientation and the creative impulses for self-expression. No other sign has such a profound instinct for survival and reproduction. Out of the abyss of emotions come a thousand creations, each one possessing a life of its own.

Scorpio is completion, determination, and endurance, fortified with enough stamina to outlive any enemy. It is the pursuit of goals despite any threat, warning, or obstacle that might stand in the way. It simply cannot be stopped. It knows when to wait and when to proceed. It is the constant state of readiness, a vibrant living force that constantly pumps out its rhythm from the depths of being.

Secretive and intimate, Scorpio symbolizes the self-directed creature with a will of steel. It is the flaming desire to create, manipulate, and control with a magician's touch. But the most mysterious quality is the capacity for metamorphosis, or total transformation.

This represents supremacy in the battle with dark unseen forces. It is the state of being totally fearless—the embodiment of truth and courage. It symbolizes the human capacity to face all danger and emerge supreme, to heal oneself. As a caterpillar spins its way into the darkness of a cocoon, Scorpio faces the end of existence, says goodbye to an old way of life, and goes through a kind of death—or total change.

Then, amid the dread of uncertainty, something remarkable happens. From hopelessness or personal crisis a new individual emerges, like a magnificent butterfly leaving behind its cocoon. It is a human being completely transformed and victorious. This is Scorpio.

SAGITTARIUS
The Sign of the Archer

Sagittarius is the sign of adventure and a thousand and one new experiences. It is the cause and purpose of every new attempt at adventure or self-understanding. It is the embodiment of enthusiasm, search for truth, and love of wisdom. Hope and optimism characterize this section of the Zodiac, and it is the ability to leave the past behind and set out again with positive resilience and a happy, cheerful outlook.

It is intelligence and exuberance, youthful idealism, and the desire to expand all horizons. It is the constant hatching of dreams, the hunger for knowledge, travel and experience. The goal is exploration itself.

Sagittarius is generosity, humor, and goodness of nature, backed up by the momentum of great expectations. It symbolizes the ability of people to be back in the race after having the most serious spills over the biggest hurdles. It is a healthy, positive outlook and the capacity to meet each new moment with unaffected buoyancy.

At this point in the Zodiac, greater conscious understanding begins to develop self-awareness and self-acceptance. It is an Olympian capacity to look upon the bright side and to evolve that aspect of mind we call conscience.

CAPRICORN
The Sign of the Sea Goat

Capricorn is the sign of structure and physical law. It rules depth, focus, and concentration. It is the symbol of success through perseverance, happiness through profundity. It is victory over disruption, and finds reality in codes set up by society and culture. It is the perpetuation of useful, tested patterns and a desire to protect what has already been established.

It is cautious, conservative, conscious of the passage of time, yet ageless. The Goat symbolizes the incorporation of reason into living and depth into loving.

Stability, responsibility, and fruitfulness through loyalty color this sector of the Zodiac with an undeniable and irrepressible awareness of success, reputation, and honor. Capricorn is the culmination of our earthly dreams, the pinnacle of our worldly life.

It is introspection and enlightenment through serious contemplation of the Self and its position in the world. It is mastery of understanding and the realization of dreams.

Capricorn is a winter blossom, a born professional with an aim of harmony and justice, beauty, grace, and success. It is the well-constructed pyramid: perfect and beautiful, architecturally correct, mysteriously implacable, and hard to know. It is highly organized and built on precise foundations to last and last and last. It is practical, useful yet magnificent and dignified, signifying permanence and careful planning. Like a pyramid, Capricorn has thick impenetrable walls, complex passageways, and false corridors. Yet somewhere at the heart of this ordered structure is the spirit of a mighty ruler.

AQUARIUS
The Sign of the Water Bearer

Aquarius is the symbol of idealized free society. It is the herding instinct in man as a social animal. It is the collection of heterogeneous elements of human consciousness in coherent peaceful coexistence. Friendship, goodwill, and harmonious contact are Aquarius attributes. It is founded on the principle of individual freedom and the brotherly love and respect for the rights of all men and women on Earth.

It is strength of will and purpose, altruism, and love of human fellowship. It is the belief in spontaneity and free choice, in the openness to live in a spirit of harmony and cooperation—liberated from restriction, repression, and conventional codes of conduct. It is the brilliant capacity to assimilate information instantaneously at the last minute and translate that information into immediate creative action, and so the result is to live in unpredictability.

This is the progressive mind, the collective mind—groups of people getting together to celebrate life. Aquarius is the child of the future, the utopian working for the betterment of the human race. Funds, charities, seeking better cities and better living conditions for others, involvement in great forms of media or communication, science or research in the hope of joining mankind to his higher self—this is all Aquarius.

It is invention, genius, revolution, discovery—instantaneous breakthrough from limitations. It's a departure from convention, eccentricity, the unexpected development that changes the course of history. It is the discovery of people and all the arteries that join them together. Aquarius is adventure, curiosity, exotic and alien appeal. It pours the water of life and intelligence for all humanity to drink. It is humanism, community, and the element of surprise.

PISCES
The Sign of the Fishes

Pisces is faith—undistracted, patient, all-forgiving faith—and therein lies the Pisces capacity for discipline, endurance, and stamina.

It is imagination and other-worldliness, the condition

of living a foggy, uncertain realm of poetry, music, and fantasy. Passive and compassionate, this sector of the Zodiac symbolizes the belief in the inevitability of life. It represents the view of life that everything exists in waves, like the sea. All reality as we know it is a dream, a magic illusion that must ultimately be washed away. Tides pull this way and that, whirlpools and undercurrents sweep across the bottom of life's existence, but in Pisces there is total acceptance of all tides, all rhythms, all possibilities. It is the final resolution of all personal contradictions and all confusing paradoxes.

It is the search for truth and honesty, and the devotion to love, utterly and unquestionably. It is the desire to act with wisdom, kindness, and responsibility and to welcome humanity completely free from scorn, malice, discrimination, or prejudice. It is total, all-embracing, idealistic love. It is the acceptance of two sides of a question at once and love through sacrifice.

Pisces is beyond reality. We are here today, but may be gone tomorrow. Let the tide of circumstances carry you where it will, for nothing is forever. As all things come, so must they go. In the final reel, all things must pass away. It is deliverance from sorrow through surrender to the infinite. The emotions are as vast as the ocean, yet in the pain of confusion there is hope in the secret cell of one's own heart. Pisces symbolizes liberation from pain through love, faith, and forgiveness.

THE SIGNS AND
THEIR KEY WORDS

		Positive	Negative
ARIES	self	courage, initiative, pioneer instinct	brash rudeness, selfish impetuosity
TAURUS	money	endurance, loyalty, wealth	obstinacy, gluttony
GEMINI	mind	versatility, communication	capriciousness, unreliability
CANCER	family	sympathy, homing instinct	clannishness, childishness
LEO	children	love, authority, integrity	egotism, force
VIRGO	work	purity, industry, analysis	faultfinding, cynicism
LIBRA	marriage	harmony, justice	vacillation, superficiality
SCORPIO	sex	survival, regeneration	vengeance, discord
SAGITTARIUS	travel	optimism, higher learning	lawlessness, irresponsibility
CAPRICORN	career	depth, responsibility	narrowness, gloom
AQUARIUS	friends	humanity, genius	perverse unpredictability
PISCES	faith	spiritual love, universality	diffusion, escapism

THE ELEMENTS AND
THE QUALITIES OF THE SIGNS

Every sign has both an element and a quality associated with it. The element indicates the basic makeup of the sign, and the quality describes the kind of activity associated with each.

Element	Sign	Quality	Sign
Fire	Aries	Cardinal	Aries
	Leo		Libra
	Sagittarius		Cancer
			Capricorn
Earth	Taurus	Fixed	Taurus
	Virgo		Leo
	Capricorn		Scorpio
			Aquarius
Air	Gemini	Mutable	Gemini
	Libra		Virgo
	Aquarius		Sagittarius
			Pisces
Water	Cancer		
	Scorpio		
	Pisces		

Signs can be grouped together according to their element and quality. Signs of the same element share many basic traits in common. They tend to form stable configurations and ultimately harmonious relationships. Signs of the same quality are often less harmonious, but share many dynamic potentials for growth and profound fulfillment.

The following pages describe these sign groupings in more detail.

The Fire Signs

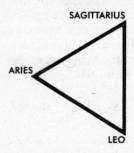

This is the fire group. On the whole these are emotional, volatile types, quick to anger, quick to forgive. They are adventurous, powerful people and act as a source of inspiration for everyone. They spark into action with immediate exuberant impulses. They are intelligent, self-involved, creative, and idealistic. They all share a certain vibrancy and glow that outwardly reflects an inner flame and passion for living.

The Earth Signs

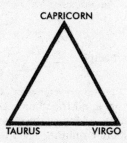

This is the earth group. They are in constant touch with the material world and tend to be conservative. Although they are all capable of spartan self-discipline, they are earthy, sensual people who are stimulated by the tangible, elegant, and luxurious. The thread of their lives is always practical, but they do fantasize and are often attracted to dark, mysterious, emotional people. They are like great cliffs overhanging the sea, forever married to the ocean but always resisting erosion from the dark, emotional forces that thunder at their feet.

The Air Signs

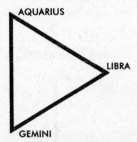

This is the air group. They are light, mental creatures desirous of contact, communication, and relationship. They are involved with people and the forming of ties on many levels. Original thinkers, they are the bearers of human news. Their language is their sense of word, color, style, and beauty. They provide an atmosphere suitable and pleasant for living. They add change and versatility to the scene, and it is through them that we can explore human intelligence and experience.

The Water Signs

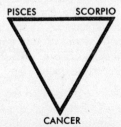

This is the water group. Through the water people, we are all joined together on emotional, nonverbal levels.

The water signs are silent, mysterious types whose magic hypnotizes even the most determined realist. They have uncanny perceptions about people and are as rich as the oceans when it comes to feeling, emotion, or imagination. They are sensitive, mystical creatures with memories that go back beyond time. Through water, life is sustained. These people have the potential for the depths of darkness or the heights of mysticism and art.

The Cardinal Signs

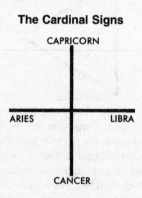

The cardinal signs present a picture of dynamism, activity, tremendous stress, and remarkable achievement. These people know the meaning of great change since their lives are often characterized by significant crises and major successes. The cardinal signs mark the beginning of the four seasons. And this combination is like a simultaneous storm of summer, fall, winter, and spring. The danger is chaotic diffusion of energy; the potential is irrepressible growth and victory.

The Fixed Signs

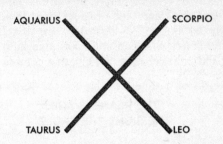

Fixed signs are always establishing themselves in a given place or area of experience. Like explorers who arrive and plant a flag, these people claim a position from which they do not enjoy being deposed. They are staunch, stalwart, upright, trusty, honorable people, although their obstinacy is well-known. Their contribution is fixity, and they are the angels who support our visible world.

The Mutable Signs

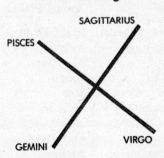

Mutable people are versatile, sensitive, intelligent, nervous, and deeply curious about life. They are the translators of all energy. They often carry out or complete tasks initiated by others. People from mutable signs have highly developed minds; they are imaginative and jumpy and think and talk a lot. At worst their lives are a Tower of Babel. At best they are adaptable and ready creatures who can assimilate one kind of experience and enjoy it while anticipating coming changes.

THE PLANETS AND
THE SIGNS THEY RULE

The signs of the Zodiac are linked to the planets in the following way. Each sign is governed or ruled by one or more planets. No matter where the planets are located in the sky at any given moment, they still rule their respective signs. When they travel through the signs they rule, they have special dignity and their effects are stronger.

Following is a list of the planets and the signs they rule. After you read the definitions of the planets from pages 88 to 96, see if you can determine how the planet ruling *your* Sun sign has affected your life.

Signs	**Ruling Planets**
Aries	Mars, Pluto
Taurus	Venus
Gemini	Mercury
Cancer	Moon
Leo	Sun
Virgo	Mercury
Libra	Venus
Scorpio	Mars, Pluto
Sagittarius	Jupiter
Capricorn	Saturn
Aquarius	Saturn, Uranus
Pisces	Jupiter, Neptune

THE ZODIAC AND
THE HUMAN BODY

The signs of the Zodiac are linked to the human body in a direct relationship. Each sign has a part of the body with which it is associated.

It is traditionally believed that surgery is best performed when the Moon is passing through a sign *other* than the sign associated with the part of the body upon which an operation is to be performed. But often the presence of the Moon in a particular sign will bring the focus of attention to that very part of the body under medical scrutiny.

The principles of medical astrology are complex and beyond the scope of this introduction. We can, however, list the signs of the Zodiac and the parts of the human body connected with them. Once you learn these correspondences, you'll be amazed at how accurate they are.

Signs	Human Body
Aries	Head, brain, face, upper jaw
Taurus	Throat, neck, lower jaw
Gemini	Hands, arms, lungs, nerves
Cancer	Stomach, breasts, womb, liver
Leo	Heart, spine
Virgo	Intestines, liver
Libra	Kidneys, lower back
Scorpio	Sex and eliminative organs
Sagittarius	Hips, thighs, liver
Capricorn	Skin, bones, teeth, knees
Aquarius	Circulatory system, lower legs
Pisces	Feet, tone of being

THE ZODIACAL HOUSES
AND THE RISING SIGN

Apart from the month and day of birth, the exact time of birth is another vital factor in the determination of an accurate horoscope. Not only do planets move with great speed, but one must know how far the Earth has turned during the day. That way you can determine exactly where the planets are located with respect to the precise birthplace of an individual. This makes your horoscope *your* horoscope.

The horoscope sets up a kind of framework around which the life of an individual grows like wild ivy, this way and that, weaving its way around the trellis of the natal positions of the planets. The year of birth tells us the positions of the distant, slow-moving planets Jupiter, Saturn, Uranus, Neptune, and Pluto. The month of birth indicates the Sun sign, or birth sign as it is commonly called, as well as indicating the positions of the rapidly moving planets Venus, Mercury, and Mars. The day of birth, as well as the time, locates the position of our Moon. And the moment of birth—the exact hour and minute—determines the houses through what is called the Ascendant, or Rising sign.

The illustration on the next page shows the flat chart, or natural wheel, an astrologer uses. The inner circle of the wheel is labeled 1 through 12. These 12 divisions are known as the houses of the Zodiac.

The 1st house always starts from the position marked E, which corresponds to the eastern horizon. The rest of the houses 2 through 12 follow around in a "counterclockwise" direction. The point where each house starts is known as a cusp, or edge.

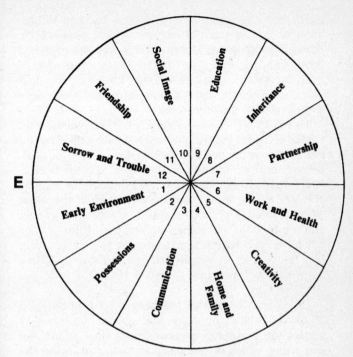

The 12 Houses of the Zodiac

The cusp, or edge, of the 1st house (point E) is where an astrologer would place your Rising sign, the Ascendant. The Rising sign is very important in a horoscope, as it defines your self-image, outlook, physical constitution, early environment, and whole orientation to life. And, as already mentioned, the exact time of your birth determines your Rising sign. Let's see how this works.

As the Earth rotates on its axis once every 24 hours, each one of the 12 signs of the Zodiac appears to be "rising" on the horizon, with a new one appearing about every two hours. Actually it is the turning of the

Earth that exposes each sign to view, but you will remember that in much of our astrological work we are discussing "apparent" motion. This Rising sign marks the Ascendant, and it colors the whole orientation of a horoscope. It indicates the sign governing the first house of the chart, and will thus determine which signs will govern all the other houses.

To visualize this idea, imagine two color wheels with twelve divisions superimposed upon each other. Just as the Zodiac is divided into twelve star groups (constellations) that we identify as the signs, another twelvefold division is used to denote the houses. Now imagine one wheel (the signs) moving slowly while the other wheel (the houses) remains still. This analogy may help you see how the signs keep shifting the "color" of the houses as the Rising sign continues to change every two hours. But to simplify things, a Table of Rising Signs has been provided on pages 20–21 for your specific Sun sign.

Once your Rising sign has been placed on the cusp of the 1st house, the signs that govern the other 11 houses can be placed on your chart. Then an astrologer, using tables of planetary motion, can locate the positions of all the planets in their appropriate houses. The house where your Sun sign is describes your basic character and your fundamental drives. And the houses where the other planets are in your chart suggest the areas of life on Earth in which you will be most likely to focus your constant energy and center your activity.

The illustration on page 83 briefly identifies each of the 12 houses of the Zodiac. Now the pages that follow provide a detailed discussion of the meanings of the houses. In the section after the houses we will define all the known planets of the solar system, with a separate section on the Moon, in order to acquaint you with more of the astrological vocabulary you will be meeting again and again.

THE MEANING OF THE HOUSES

The twelve houses of every horoscope represent areas of life on Earth, or regions of worldly experience. Depending on which sign of the Zodiac was rising on the eastern horizon at the moment of birth, the activity of each house will be "colored" by the zodiacal sign on its cusp, or edge. In other words, the sign falling on the first house will determine what signs will fall on the rest of the houses.

1 The first house determines the basic orientation to all of life on Earth. It indicates the body type, face, head, and brain. It rules your self-image, or the way others see you because of the way you see your self. This is the Ascendant of the horoscope and is the focus of energies of your whole chart. It acts like a prism through which all of the planetary light passes and is reflected in your life. It colors your outlook and influences everything you do and see.

2 This is the house of finances. Here is your approach to money and materialism in general. It indicates where the best sources are for you to improve your financial condition and your earning power as a whole. It indicates chances for gain or loss. It describes your values, alliances, and assets.

3 This is the house of the day-to-day mind. Short trips, communication, and transportation are associated with this house. It deals with routines, brothers and sisters, relatives, neighbors, and the near environment at hand. Language, letters, and the tools for transmitting information are included in third-house matters.

4 This is the house that describes your home and home life, parents, and childhood in the sense of indicating the kind of roots you come from. It symbolizes your present home and domestic situation and reflects your need for privacy and retreat from the world, indicating, of course, what kind of scene you require.

5 Pleasure, love affairs, amusements, parties, creativity, children. This is the house of passion and courtship and of expressing your talents, whatever they are. It is related to the development of your personal life and the capacity to express feeling and enjoy romance.

6 This is the house of work. Here there are tasks to be accomplished and maladjustments to be corrected. It is the house of health as well, and describes some of the likely places where physical health difficulties may appear. It rules routines, regimen, necessary jobs as opposed to a chosen career, army, navy, police—people employed, co-workers, and those in service to others. It indicates the individual's ability to harvest the fruit of his own efforts.

7 This is the house of marriage, partnership, and unions. It represents the alter ego, all people other than yourself, open confrontation with the public. It describes your partner and the condition of partnership as you discern it. In short, it is your "take" on the world. It indicates your capacity to make the transition from courtship to marriage and specifically what you seek out in others.

8 This is the house of deep personal transition, sex as a form of mutual surrender and interchange between human beings. It is the release from tensions and the completion of the creative processes. The eighth house also has to do with taxes, inheritances, and the finances of others, as well as death as the ending of cycles and crises.

9 This is the house of the higher mind, philosophy, religion, and the expression of personal conscience through moral codes. It indicates political leanings, ethical views, and the capacity of the individual for a broader perspective and deeper understanding of himself in relation to society. It is through the ninth house that you make great strides in learning and travel to distant places and come to know yourself through study, dreams, and wide experience.

10 This is the house of career, honor, and prestige. It marks the culmination of worldly experience and indicates the highest point you can reach, what you look up to, and how high you can go in this lifetime. It describes your parents, employers, and how you view authority figures, the condition and direction of your profession, and your position in the community.

11 This is the house of friendships. It describes your social behavior, your views on humanity, and your hopes, aspirations, and wishes for an ideal life. It will indicate what kinds of groups, clubs, organizations, and friendships you tend to form and what you seek out in your chosen alliances other than with your mate or siblings. This house suggests the capacity for the freedom and unconventionality that an individual is seeking, his sense of his connection with mankind, and the definition of his goals, personal and social.

12 This is the house of seclusion, secret wisdom, and self-incarceration. It indicates our secret enemies as well, in the sense that there may be persons, feelings, or memories we are trying to escape. It is self-undoing in that this house acts against the ego in order to find a higher, more universal purpose. It rules prisons, hospitals, charities, and selfless service. It is the house of unfinished psychic business.

THE PLANETS OF THE SOLAR SYSTEM

The planets of the solar system all travel around the Sun at different speeds and different distances. Taken with the Sun, they all distribute individual intelligence and ability throughout the entire chart.

The planets modify the influence of the Sun in a chart according to their own particular natures, strengths, and positions. Their positions must be calculated for each year and day, and their function and expression in a horoscope will change as they move from one area of the Zodiac to another.

Following, you will find brief statements of their pure meanings.

THE SUN

The Sun is the center of existence. Around this flaming sphere all the planets revolve in endless orbits. Our star is constantly sending out its beams of light and energy without which no life on Earth would be possible. In astrology it symbolizes everything we are trying to become, the center around which all of our activity in life will always revolve. It is the symbol of our basic nature and describes the natural and constant thread that runs through everything that we do from birth to death on this planet.

Everything in the horoscope ultimately revolves around this singular body. Although other forces may be prominent in the charts of some individuals, still the

THE SUN

Sun is the total nucleus of being and symbolizes the complete potential of every human being alive. It is vitality and the life force. Your whole essence comes from the position of the Sun.

You are always trying to express the Sun according to its position by house and sign. Possibility for all development is found in the Sun, and it marks the fundamental character of your personal radiations all around you.

It symbolizes strength, vigor, ardor, generosity, and the ability to function effectively as a mature individual and a creative force in society. It is consciousness of the gift of life. The undeveloped solar nature is arrogant pushy, undependable, and proud, and is constantly using force.

MERCURY

Mercury is the planet closest to the Sun. It races around our star, gathering information and translating it to the rest of the system. Mercury represents your capacity to understand the desires of your own will and to translate those desires into action.

MERCURY

In other words it is the planet of mind and the power of communication. Through Mercury we develop an ability to think, write, speak, and observe—to become aware of the world around us. It colors our attitudes and vision of the world, as well as our capacity to communicate our inner responses to the outside world. Some people who have serious disabilities in their power of verbal communication have often wrongly been described as people lacking intelligence.

Although this planet (and its position in the horoscope) indicates your power to communicate your thoughts and perceptions to the world, intelligence is something deeper. Intelligence is distributed throughout all the planets. It is the relationship of the planets to each other that truly describes what we call intelligence. Mercury rules speaking, language, mathematics, draft and design, students, messengers, young people, offices, teachers, and any pursuits where the mind of man has wings.

VENUS

Venus is beauty. It symbolizes the harmony and radiance of a rare and elusive quality: beauty itself. It is refinement and delicacy, softness and charm. In astrology it indicates grace, balance, and the aesthetic sense. Where Venus is we see beauty, a gentle drawing in of energy and the need for satisfaction and completion. It is a special touch that finishes off rough edges.

VENUS

Venus is the planet of sensitivity and affection, and it is always the place for that other elusive phenomenon: love. Venus describes our sense of what is beautiful and loving. Poorly developed, it is vulgar, tasteless, and self-indulgent. But its ideal is the flame of spiritual love—Aphrodite, goddess of love, and the sweetness and power of personal beauty.

MARS

Mars is raw, crude energy. The planet next to Earth but outward from the Sun is a fiery red sphere that charges through the horoscope with force and fury. It represents the way you reach out for new adventure and new experience. It is energy drive, initiative, courage, daring. It is the power to start something and see it through. It can be thoughtless, cruel and wild, angry and hostile, causing cuts, burns, scalds, wounds. It can stab its way through a chart, or it can be the symbol of healthy spirited adventure, well-channeled constructive power to begin and keep up the drive.

MARS

If you have trouble starting things, if you lack the get-up-and-go to start the ball rolling, if you lack aggressiveness and self-confidence, chances are there's another planet influencing your Mars. Mars rules soldiers, butchers, surgeons, salespeople—in general any field that requires daring, bold skill, operational technique, or self-promotion.

JUPITER

Jupiter is the largest planet of the solar system. Planet Jupiter rules good luck and good cheer, health, wealth, optimism, happiness, success, joy. It is the symbol of opportunity and always opens the way for new possibilities in your life. It rules exuberance, enthusiasm, wisdom, knowledge, generosity, and all forms of expansion in general. It rules actors, statesmen, clerics, professional people, religion, publishing, and the distribution of many people over large areas.

JUPITER

Sometimes Jupiter makes you think you deserve everything, and you become sloppy, wasteful, careless and rude, prodigal and lawless, in the illusion that nothing can ever go wrong. Then there is the danger of your showing overconfidence, exaggeration, undependability, and overindulgence.

Jupiter is the minimization of limitation and the emphasis on spirituality and potential. It is the thirst for knowledge and higher learning.

SATURN

Saturn circles our system in dark splendor with its mysterious rings, forcing us to be awakened to whatever we have neglected in the past. It will present real puzzles and problems to be solved, causing delays, obstacles, and hindrances. By doing so, Saturn stirs our own sensitivity to those areas where we are laziest.

SATURN

Here we must patiently develop method, and only through painstaking effort can our ends be achieved. It brings order to a horoscope and imposes reason just where we are feeling least reasonable. By creating limitations and boundary, Saturn shows the consequences of being human and demands that we accept the changing cycles inevitable in human life. Saturn rules time, old age, and sobriety. It can bring depression, gloom, jealousy, and greed, or serious acceptance of responsibilities out of which success will develop. With Saturn there is nothing to do but face facts. It rules laborers, stones, granite, rocks, and crystals.

THE OUTER PLANETS: URANUS, NEPTUNE, PLUTO

Uranus, Neptune, and Pluto are the outer planets. They liberate human beings from cultural conditioning, and in that sense are the lawbreakers. In early times it was thought that Saturn was the last planet of the solar system—the outer limit beyond which we could never go. The discovery of the next three planets beyond Saturn ushered in new phases of human history, revolution, and technology.

URANUS

Uranus rules unexpected change, upheaval, revolution. It is the symbol of total independence and asserts the freedom of an individual from all restriction and restraint. It is a breakthrough planet and indicates talent, originality, and genius in a horoscope. It usually causes last-minute reversals and changes of plan, unwanted separations, accidents, catastrophes, and eccentric behavior. It can add irrational rebelliousness and perverse bohemianism to a personality or a streak of unaffected brilliance in science and art.

URANUS

Uranus rules technology, aviation, and all forms of electrical and electronic advancement. It governs great leaps forward and topsy-turvy situations, and always turns things around at the last minute. Its effects are difficult to predict, since it rules sudden last-minute decisions and events that come like lightning out of the blue.

NEPTUNE

Neptune dissolves existing reality the way the sea erodes the cliffs beside it. Its effects are subtle like the ringing of a buoy's bell in the fog. It suggests a reality higher than definition can usually describe. It awakens a sense of higher responsibility often causing guilt, worry, anxieties, or delusions. Neptune is associated with all forms of escape and can make things seem a certain way so convincingly that you are absolutely sure of something that eventually turns out to be quite different.

NEPTUNE

It is the planet of illusion and therefore governs the invisible realms that lie beyond our ordinary minds, beyond our simple factual ability to prove what is "real." Treachery, deceit, disillusionment, and disappointment are linked to Neptune. It describes a vague reality that promises eternity and the divine, yet in a manner so complex that we cannot really fathom it at all. At its worst Neptune is a cheap intoxicant; at its best it is the poetry, music, and inspiration of the higher planes of spiritual love. It has dominion over movies, photographs, and much of the arts.

PLUTO

Pluto lies at the outpost of our system and therefore rules finality in a horoscope—the final closing of chapters in your life, the passing of major milestones and points of development from which there is no return. It is a final wipeout, a closeout, an evacuation. It is a subtle but powerful catalyst in all transformations that occur. It creates, destroys, then recreates. Sometimes Pluto starts its influence with a minor event or insignificant incident that might even go unnoticed. Slowly but surely, little by little, everything changes, until at last there has been a total transformation in the area of your life where Pluto has been operating. It rules mass thinking and the trends that society first rejects, then adopts, and finally outgrows.

PLUTO

Pluto rules the dead and the underworld—all the powerful forces of creation and destruction that go on all the time beneath, around, and above us. It can bring a lust for power with strong obsessions.

It is the planet that rules the metamorphosis of the caterpillar into a butterfly, for it symbolizes the capacity to change totally and forever a person's lifestyle, way of thought, and behavior.

THE MOON

Exactly how does the Moon affect us psychologically and psychically? We know it controls the tides. We understand how it affects blood rhythm and body tides, together with all the chemical fluids that constitute our physical selves. Astronauts have walked upon its surface, and our scientists are now studying and analyzing data that will help determine the age of our satellite, its origin, and makeup.

THE MOON

But the true mystery of that small body as it circles our Earth each month remains hidden. Is it really a dead, lifeless body that has no light or heat of its own, reflecting only what the gigantic Sun throws toward it? Is it a sensitive reflecting device, which translates the blinding, billowing energy from our star into a language our bodies can understand?

In astrology, the Moon is said to rule our feelings, customs, habits, and moods. As the Sun is the constant, ever shining source of life in daytime, the Moon is our nighttime mother, lighting up the night and swiftly moving, reflecting ever so rapidly the changing phases of behavior and personality. If we feel happy or joyous, or we notice certain habits and repetitive feelings that bubble up from our dark centers then vanish as quickly as they appeared, very often it is the position of the Moon that describes these changes.

THE MOON IN ALL SIGNS

The Moon moves quickly through the Zodiac, that is, through all twelve signs of our Sun's apparent path. It stays in each sign for about 2¼ days. During its brief stay in a given sign, the moods and responses of people are always colored by the nature of that sign, any planets located there at that time, or any other heavenly bodies placed in such a way that the Moon will pick up their "vibration" as well. It's astonishing to observe how clearly the Moon changes people's interests and involvements as it moves along.

The following section gives brief descriptions of the Moon's influence in each sign.

MOON IN ARIES

There's excitement in the air. Some new little thing appears, and people are quick and full of energy and enterprise, ready for something new and turning on to a new experience. There's not much patience or hesitation, doubt or preoccupation with guilty self-damning recriminations. What's needed is action. People feel like putting their plans into operation. Pleasure and adventure characterize the mood, and it's time for things to change, pick up, improve. Confidence, optimism, positive feeling pervade the air. Sick people take a turn for the better. Life stirs with a feeling of renewal. People react bravely to challenges, with a sense of courage and dynamism. Self-reliance is the key word, and people minimize their problems and maximize the power to exercise freedom of the will. There is an air of abruptness and shortness of consideration, as people are feeling the courage of their convictions to do something for themselves. Feelings are strong and intuitive, and the mood is idealistic and freedom-oriented.

MOON IN TAURUS

Here the mood is just as pleasure loving, but less idealistic. Now the concerns are more materialistic, money-oriented, down-to-earth. The mood is stable, diligent, thoughtful, deliberate. It is a time when feelings are rich and deep, with a profound appreciation of the good things the world has to offer and the pleasures of the sensations. It is a period when people's minds are serious, realistic, and devoted to the increases and improvements of property and possessions and acquisition of wealth. There is a conservative tone, and people are fixed in their views, needing to add to their stability in every way. Assessment of assets, criticism, and the execution of tasks are strong involvements of the Taurus Moon when financial matters demand attention. It is devotion to security on a financial and emotional level. It is a fertile time, when ideas can begin to take root and grow.

MOON IN GEMINI

There is a rapid increase in movement. People are going places, exchanging ideas and information. Gossip and news travel fast under a Gemini Moon, because people are naturally involved with communication, finding out things from some, passing on information to others. Feelings shift to a mental level now, and people feel and say things that are sincere at the moment but lack the root and depth to endure much beyond the moment. People are involved with short-term engagements, quick trips. There is a definite need for changing the scene. You'll find people flirtatious and talkative, experimental and easygoing, falling into encounters they hadn't planned on. The mind is quick and active, with powers of writing and speaking greatly enhanced. Radio, television, letters, newspapers, magazines are in the spotlight with the Moon in Gemini, and new chances pop up for self-expression, with new people involved. Relatives and neighbors are tuned in to you and you to them. Take advantage of this fluidity of mind. It can rescue you from worldly involvements and get you into new surroundings for a short while.

MOON IN CANCER

Now you'll see people heading home. People turn their attention inward to their place of residence under a Cancer Moon. The active, changeable moods of yesterday vanish, and people settle in as if they were searching for a nest of security. Actually people are retiring, seeking to find peace and quiet within themselves. That's what they're feeling when they prefer to stay home rather than go out with a crowd of people to strange places. They need the warmth and comfort of the family and hearth. Maybe they feel anxious and insecure from the hustle and bustle of the workaday world. Maybe they're just tired. But it's definitely a time of tender need for emotional sustenance. It's a time for nostalgia and returning to times and places that once nourished deeply. Thoughts of parents, family, and old associations come to people. The heritage of their family ties holds them strongly now. These are personal needs that must be fed. Moods are deep and mysterious and sometimes sad. People are silent, psychic, and imaginative during this period. It's a fruitful time when people respond to love, food, and all the comforts of the inner world.

MOON IN LEO

The shift is back out in the world, and people are born again, like kids. They feel zestful, passionate, exuberant and need plenty of attention. They're interested in having a good time, enjoying themselves, and the world of entertainment takes over for a while. Places of amusement, theaters, parties, sprees, a whole gala of glamorous events, characterize this stage of the Moon's travel. Gracious, lavish hosting and a general feeling of buoyancy and flamboyancy are in the air. It's a time of sunny, youthful fun when people are in the mood to take chances and win. The approach is direct, ardent, and strong. Bossy, authoritarian feelings predominate, and people throw themselves forward for all they're worth. Flattery is rampant, but the ego is vibrant and flourishing with the kiss of life, romance, and love. Speculation is indicated, and it's usually a time to go out and try your hand at love. Life is full and rich as a summer meadow, and feelings are warm.

MOON IN VIRGO

The party's over. Eyelashes are on the table. This is a time for cleaning up after the merrymakers have gone home. People are now concerned with sobering up and getting personal affairs straight, clearing up any confusions or undefined feelings from the night before, and generally attending to the practical business of doctoring up after the party. People are back at work, concerned with necessary, perhaps tedious tasks—paying bills, fixing and adjusting things, and generally purifying their lives, streamlining their affairs, and involving themselves with work and service to the community. Purity is the key word in personal habits, diet, and emotional needs. Propriety and coolness take the place of yesterday's devil-may-care passion, and the results are a detached, inhibited period under a Virgo

Moon. Feelings are not omitted; they are merely subjected to the scrutiny of the mind and thus purified. Health comes to the fore, and people are interested in clearing up problems.

MOON IN LIBRA

Here there is a mood of harmony, when people strive to join with other people in a bond of peace and justice. At this time people need relationships and often seek the company of others in a smooth-flowing feeling of love, beauty, and togetherness. People make efforts to understand other people, and though it's not the best time to make decisions, many situations keep presenting themselves from the outside to change plans and offer new opportunities. There is a general search for accord between partners, and differences are explored as similarities are shared. The tone is concilatory, and the mood is one of cooperation, patience, and tolerance. People do not generally feel independent, and sometimes this need to share or lean on others disturbs them. It shouldn't. This is the moment for uniting and sharing, for feeling a mutual flow of kindness and tenderness between people. The air is ingratiating and sometimes lacks stamina, courage, and a consistent, definite point of view. But it is a time favoring the condition of beauty and the development of all forms of art.

MOON IN SCORPIO

This is not a mood of sharing. It's driving, intense, brooding—full of passion and desire. Its baser aspects are the impulses of selfishness, cruelty, and the pursuit of animal drives and appetites. There is a craving for excitement and a desire to battle and win in a bloodthirsty war for survival. It is competitive and ruthless, sarcastic and easily bruised, highly sexual and touchy, without being especially tender. Retaliation, jealousy, and revenge can be felt too during this time. Financial involvements, debts, and property issues arise now. Powerful underworld forces are at work here, and great care is needed to transform ignorance into wisdom, to keep the mind from descending into the lower depths. During the Moon's stay in Scorpio we contact the dark undercurrents swirling around and get in touch with a magical part of our natures. Interest lies in death, inheritance, and the powers of rebirth and regeneration.

MOON IN SAGITTARIUS

Here the mind climbs out of the depths, and people are involved with the higher, more enlightened, and conscious facets of their personality. There's a renewed interest in learning, education, and philosophy, and a new involvement with ethics, morals, national and international issues: a concern with looking for a better way to live. It's a time of general improvement, with people feeling more deeply hopeful and optimistic. They are dreaming of new places, new possibilities, new horizons. They are emerging from the abyss and leaving the past behind, with their eyes gazing toward the new horizon. They decide to travel, or renew their contacts with those far away. They question their religious beliefs and investigate new areas of metaphysical inquiry. It's a time for adventure, sports, playing the field—people have their eye on new possibilities. They are bored with depression and details. They feel restless and optimistic, joyous and delighted to be alive. Thoughts revolve around adventure, travel, liberation.

MOON IN CAPRICORN

When the Moon moves into Capricorn, things slow down considerably. People require a quiet, organized, and regularized condition. Their minds are sober and realistic, and they are methodically going about bringing their dreams and plans into reality. They are more conscious of what is standing between them and success, and during this time they take definite, decisive steps to remove any obstacles from their path. They are cautious, suspicious, sometimes depressed, discouraged, and gloomy, but they are more determined than ever to accomplish their tasks. They take care of responsibilities now, wake up to facts, and wrestle with problems and dilemmas of this world. They are politically minded and concerned with social convention now, and it is under a Capricorn Moon that conditioning and conformity elicit the greatest responses. People are moderate and serious and surround themselves with what is most familiar. They want predictable situations and need time to think deeply and deliberately about all issues. It's a time for planning.

MOON IN AQUARIUS

Spontaneity replaces the sober predictability of yesterday. Now events, people, and situations pop up, and you take advantage of unsought opportunities and can expect the unexpected. Surprises, reversals, and shifts in plans mark this period. There is a resurgence of optimism, and things you wouldn't expect to happen suddenly do. What you were absolutely sure was going to happen simply doesn't. Here there is a need for adventure born from a healthy curiosity that characterizes people's moods. Unrealistic utopias are dreamed of, and it is from such idealistic dreams that worlds of the future are built. There is a renewed interest in friendship, comradeship, community, and union on high planes of mental and spiritual companionship. People free each other from grudges or long-standing deadlocks, and there is a hopeful joining of hands in a spirit of love and peace. People don't feel like sticking to previous plans, and they must be able to respond to new situations at the last minute. People need freedom. Groups of people come together and meet, perhaps for a common purpose of having dinner or hearing music, and leave knowing each other better.

MOON IN PISCES

Flashes of brilliant insight and mysterious knowledge characterize the Moon's passage in Pisces. Sometimes valuable "truths" seem to emerge which, later in the light of day, turn out to be false. This is a time of poetry, intuition, and music, when worldly realities can be the most illusory and unreliable of all. There are often feelings of remorse, guilt, or sorrow connected with a Pisces Moon—sorrow from the childhood or family or past. Confusion, anxiety, worry, and a host of imagined pains and sorrows may drag you down until you cannot move or think. Often there are connections with hospitals, prisons, alcohol, drugs, and lower forms of escape. It is a highly emotional time, when the feelings and compassion for humanity and all people everywhere rise to the surface of your being. Mysteries of society and the soul now rise to demand solutions, but often the riddles posed during this period have many answers that all seem right. It is more a time for inner reflection than positive action. It is a time when poetry and music float to the surface of the being, and for the creative artist it is the richest source of inspiration.

MOON TABLES

CORRECTION FOR NEW YORK TIME, FIVE HOURS WEST OF GREENWICH

Atlanta, Boston, Detroit, Miami, Washington, Montreal,
Ottawa, Quebec, Bogota,
Havana, Lima, Santiago...................... Same time

Chicago, New Orleans, Houston, Winnipeg, Churchill,
Mexico City.............................. Deduct 1 hour

Albuquerque, Denver, Phoenix, El Paso, Edmonton,
Helena.................................... Deduct 2 hours

Los Angeles, San Francisco, Reno, Portland,
Seattle, Vancouver....................... Deduct 3 hours

Honolulu, Anchorage, Fairbanks, Kodiak... Deduct 5 hours

Nome, Samoa, Tonga, Midway .... Deduct 6 hours

Halifax, Bermuda, San Juan, Caracas, La Paz,
Barbados .... Add 1 hour

St. John's, Brasilia, Rio de Janeiro, Sao Paulo,
Buenos Aires, Montevideo.................. Add 2 hours

Azores, Cape Verde Islands.................... Add 3 hours

Canary Islands, Madeira, Reykjavik .... Add 4 hours

London, Paris, Amsterdam, Madrid, Lisbon,
Gibraltar, Belfast, Rabat .... Add 5 hours

Frankfurt, Rome, Oslo, Stockholm, Prague,
Belgrade..................................... Add 6 hours

Bucharest, Beirut, Tel Aviv, Athens, Istanbul, Cairo,
Alexandria, Cape Town, Johannesburg...... Add 7 hours

Moscow, Leningrad, Baghdad, Dhahran,
Addis Ababa, Nairobi, Teheran, Zanzibar... Add 8 hours

Bombay, Calcutta, Sri Lanka .... Add 10 ½ hours

Hong Kong, Shanghai, Manila, Peking,
Perth .... Add 13 hours

Tokyo, Okinawa, Darwin, Pusan .... Add 14 hours

Sydney, Melbourne, Port Moresby, Guam .... Add 15 hours

Auckland, Wellington, Suva, Wake........... Add 17 hours

2002 MOON SIGN DATES—NEW YORK TIME

JANUARY		FEBRUARY		MARCH	
Day Moon Enters		Day Moon Enters		Day Moon Enters	
1. Leo		1. Libra	3:45 am	1. Libra	
2. Virgo	6:35 pm	2. Libra		2. Scorp.	1:52 pm
3. Virgo		3. Scorp.	5:36 am	3. Scorp.	
4. Libra	8:25 pm	4. Scorp.		4. Sagitt.	4:56 pm
5. Libra		5. Sagitt.	10:22 am	5. Sagitt.	
6. Scorp.	11:42 pm	6. Sagitt.		6. Capric.	11:49 pm
7. Scorp.		7. Capric.	6:09 pm	7. Capric.	
8. Scorp.		8. Capric.		8. Capric.	
9. Sagitt.	4:58 am	9. Capric.		9. Aquar.	9:57 am
10. Sagitt.		10. Aquar.	4:16 am	10. Aquar.	
11. Capric.	12:19 pm	11. Aquar.		11. Pisces	9:57 pm
12. Capric.		12. Pisces	3:54 pm	12. Pisces	
13. Aquar.	9:42 pm	13. Pisces		13. Pisces	
14. Aquar.		14. Pisces		14. Aries	10:35 am
15. Aquar.		15. Aries	4:27 am	15. Aries	
16. Pisces	9:01 am	16. Aries		16. Taurus	11:02 pm
17. Pisces		17. Taurus	4:59 pm	17. Taurus	
18. Aries	9:36 pm	18. Taurus		18. Taurus	
19. Aries		19. Taurus		19. Gemini	10:21 am
20. Aries		20. Gemini	3:51 am	20. Gemini	
21. Taurus	9:48 am	21. Gemini		21. Cancer	7:07 pm
22. Taurus		22. Cancer	11:17 am	22. Cancer	
23. Gemini	7:29 pm	23. Cancer		23. Cancer	
24. Gemini		24. Leo	2:37 pm	24. Leo	0:14 am
25. Gemini		25. Leo		25. Leo	
26. Cancer	1:18 am	26. Virgo	2:48 pm	26. Virgo	1:45 am
27. Cancer		27. Virgo		27. Virgo	
28. Leo	3:32 am	28. Libra	1:48 pm	28. Libra	1:05 am
29. Leo				29. Libra	
30. Virgo	3:41 am			30. Scorp.	0:22 am
31. Virgo				31. Scorp.	

Summer time to be considered where applicable.

2002 MOON SIGN DATES—NEW YORK TIME

APRIL		MAY		JUNE	
Day Moon Enters		**Day Moon Enters**		**Day Moon Enters**	
1. Sagitt.	1:49 am	1. Capric.		1. Pisces	6:38 pm
2. Sagitt.		2. Aquar.	11:45 pm	2. Pisces	
3. Capric.	6:59 am	3. Aquar.		3. Pisces	
4. Capric.		4. Aquar.		4. Aries	6:52 am
5. Aquar.	4:08 pm	5. Pisces	10:47 am	5. Aries	
6. Aquar.		6. Pisces		6. Taurus	7:08 pm
7. Aquar.		7. Aries	11:23 pm	7. Taurus	
8. Pisces	3:59 am	8. Aries		8. Taurus	
9. Pisces		9. Aries		9. Gemini	5:30 am
10. Aries	4:42 pm	10. Taurus	11:33 am	10. Gemini	
11. Aries		11. Taurus		11. Cancer	1:16 pm
12. Aries		12. Gemini	10:05 pm	12. Cancer	
13. Taurus	4:56 am	13. Gemini		13. Leo	6:40 pm
14. Taurus		14. Gemini		14. Leo	
15. Gemini	3:57 pm	15. Cancer	6:34 am	15. Virgo	10:25 pm
16. Gemini		16. Cancer		16. Virgo	
17. Gemini		17. Leo	12:53 pm	17. Virgo	
18. Cancer	1:02 am	18. Leo		18. Libra	1:12 am
19. Cancer		19. Virgo	5:01 pm	19. Libra	
20. Leo	7:22 am	20. Virgo		20. Scorp.	3:43 am
21. Leo		21. Libra	7:20 pm	21. Scorp.	
22. Virgo	10:36 am	22. Libra		22. Sagitt.	6:43 am
23. Virgo		23. Scorp.	8:39 pm	23. Sagitt.	
24. Libra	11:23 am	24. Scorp.		24. Capric.	11:02 am
25. Libra		25. Sagitt.	10:21 pm	25. Capric.	
26. Scorp.	11:16 am	26. Sagitt.		26. Aquar.	5:37 pm
27. Scorp.		27. Sagitt.		27. Aquar.	
28. Sagitt.	12:14 pm	28. Capric.	1:55 am	28. Aquar.	
29. Sagitt.		29. Capric.		29. Pisces	3:02 am
30. Capric.	4:04 pm	30. Aquar.	8:36 am	30. Pisces	
		31. Aquar.			

Summer time to be considered where applicable.

2002 MOON SIGN DATES—NEW YORK TIME

JULY Day Moon Enters		AUGUST Day Moon Enters		SEPTEMBER Day Moon Enters	
1. Aries	2:50 pm	1. Taurus		1. Cancer	4:15 pm
2. Aries		2. Gemini	10:48 pm	2. Cancer	
3. Aries		3. Gemini		3. Leo	9:38 pm
4. Taurus	3:17 am	4. Gemini		4. Leo	
5. Taurus		5. Cancer	7:03 am	5. Virgo	11:17 pm
6. Gemini	2:02 pm	6. Cancer		6. Virgo	
7. Gemini		7. Leo	11:28 am	7. Libra	10:58 pm
8. Cancer	9:38 pm	8. Leo		8. Libra	
9. Cancer		9. Virgo	1:04 pm	9. Scorp.	10:49 pm
10. Cancer		10. Virgo		10. Scorp.	
11. Leo	2:09 am	11. Libra	1:39 pm	11. Scorp.	
12. Leo		12. Libra		12. Sagitt.	0:45 am
13. Virgo	4:42 am	13. Scorp.	3:02 pm	13. Sagitt.	
14. Virgo		14. Scorp.		14. Capric.	5:49 am
15. Libra	6:40 am	15. Sagitt.	6:26 pm	15. Capric.	
16. Libra		16. Sagitt.		16. Aquar.	1:55 pm
17. Scorp.	9:14 am	17. Sagitt.		17. Aquar.	
18. Scorp.		18. Capric.	0:16 am	18. Aquar.	
19. Sagitt.	1:03 pm	19. Capric.		19. Pisces	0:19 am
20. Sagitt.		20. Aquar.	8:18 am	20. Pisces	
21. Capric.	6:27 pm	21. Aquar.		21. Aries	12:12 pm
22. Capric.		22. Pisces	6:12 pm	22. Aries	
23. Capric.		23. Pisces		23. Aries	
24. Aquar.	1:41 am	24. Pisces		24. Taurus	0:56 am
25. Aquar.		25. Aries	5:49 am	25. Taurus	
26. Pisces	11:05 am	26. Aries		26. Gemini	1:28 pm
27. Pisces		27. Taurus	6:33 pm	27. Gemini	
28. Aries	10:40 pm	28. Taurus		28. Gemini	
29. Aries		29. Taurus		29. Cancer	0:03 am
30. Aries		30. Gemini	6:46 pm	30. Cancer	
31. Taurus	11:18 am	31. Gemini			

Summer time to be considered where applicable.

2002 MOON SIGN DATES—NEW YORK TIME

OCTOBER		NOVEMBER		DECEMBER	
Day Moon Enters		**Day Moon Enters**		**Day Moon Enters**	
1. Leo	6:59 am	1. Libra	8:29 pm	1. Scorp.	6:16 am
2. Leo		2. Libra		2. Scorp.	
3. Virgo	9:53 am	3. Scorp.	8:11 pm	3. Sagitt.	6:59 am
4. Virgo		4. Scorp.		4. Sagitt.	
5. Libra	9:52 am	5. Sagitt.	8:02 pm	5. Capric.	8:40 am
6. Libra		6. Sagitt.		6. Capric.	
7. Scorp.	8:58 am	7. Capric.	10:00 pm	7. Aquar.	12:55 pm
8. Scorp.		8. Capric.		8. Aquar.	
9. Sagitt.	9:22 am	9. Capric.		9. Pisces	8:47 pm
10. Sagitt.		10. Aquar.	3:28 am	10. Pisces	
11. Capric.	12:46 pm	11. Aquar.		11. Pisces	
12. Capric.		12. Pisces	12:43 pm	12. Aries	7:59 am
13. Aquar.	7:52 pm	13. Pisces		13. Aries	
14. Aquar.		14. Pisces		14. Taurus	8:44 pm
15. Aquar.		15. Aries	0:39 am	15. Taurus	
16. Pisces	6:08 am	16. Aries		16. Taurus	
17. Pisces		17. Taurus	1:25 pm	17. Gemini	8:44 am
18. Aries	6:15 pm	18. Taurus		18. Gemini	
19. Aries		19. Taurus		19. Cancer	6:31 pm
20. Aries		20. Gemini	1:26 am	20. Cancer	
21. Taurus	6:58 am	21. Gemini		21. Cancer	
22. Taurus		22. Cancer	11:49 am	22. Leo	1:49 am
23. Gemini	7:18 pm	23. Cancer		23. Leo	
24. Gemini		24. Leo	8:01 pm	24. Virgo	7:06 am
25. Gemini		25. Leo		25. Virgo	
26. Cancer	6:11 am	26. Leo		26. Libra	10:54 am
27. Cancer		27. Virgo	1:43 am	27. Libra	
28. Leo	2:21 pm	28. Virgo		28. Scorp.	1:42 pm
29. Leo		29. Libra	4:55 am	29. Scorp.	
30. Virgo	7:00 pm	30. Libra		30. Sagitt.	4:02 pm
31. Virgo				31. Sagitt.	

Summer time to be considered where applicable.

2002 FISHING GUIDE

	Good	Best
January	1-2-21-25-28-29-30-31	6-13-26-27
February	12-20-24-25-26-27-28	4
March	6-14-25-26-27	1-2-22-28-29-30-31
April	12-20-24-28-29-30	4-25-26-27
May	4-19-26-27	12-23-24-25-28-29
June	10-22-23-24-27	3-18-21-25-26
July	2-21-24-25-26	10-17-22-23-27
August	8-20-21-22-25-31	1-15-19-23-24
September	7-13-18-21-22-23	19-20-24-29
October	19-20-21-24-29	6-13-18-22-23
November	11-17-20-21-22-27	4-18-19-23
December	4-17-18-19-22	11-16-20-21-27

2002 PLANTING GUIDE

	Aboveground Crops	Root Crops
January	17-18-22-23-26-27	5-6-7-8-12
February	13-14-18-19-23	1-2-3-4-8-9
March	17-18-22-23-26-27	1-2-3-7-8-12-13-29-30-31
April	13-14-18-19-25-26	4-8-9-27
May	16-22-23-24-25	1-2-6-7-11-28-29
June	12-13-18-19-20-21	2-3-7-8-25-26-29-30
July	16-17-18-22-23	4-5-9-27-28
August	12-13-14-15-18-19	1-2-6-23-24-28-29
September	8-9-10-11-15-19-20	2-3-24-25-29-30
October	7-8-12-13-17-18	22-23-27
November	5-8-9-13-14-18-19	2-3-23-24-29-30
December	6-10-11-15-16	1-2-20-21-27-28-29

	Pruning	Weeds and Pests
January	7-8	1-2-3-4-9-10-29-30-31
February	4	6-7-10-11-27
March	3-12-13-30-31	5-6-10-11
April	8-9-27	1-2-6-7-11-29
May	6-7	3-4-8-9-27-31
June	2-3-29-30	5-6-10-27-28
July	9-27-28	2-3-7-8-24-25-29-30
August	6-23-24	3-4-26-27-31
September	23-29-30	4-5-6-22-23-27-28
October	27	2-3-4-24-25-29-30-31
November	23-24	1-20-21-25-26-27-28
December	2-20-21-29	22-23-24-25-31

2002 PHASES OF THE MOON—NEW YORK TIME

New Moon	First Quarter	Full Moon	Last Quarter
Dec. 14 ('01)	Dec. 22 ('01)	Dec. 30 ('01)	Jan. 5
Jan. 13	Jan. 21	Jan. 28	Feb. 4
Feb. 12	Feb. 19	Feb. 27	March 5
March 13	March 21	March 28	April 3
April 12	April 20	April 26	May 4
May 12	May 19	May 26	June 3
June 10	June 18	June 24	July 2
July 10	July 16	July 24	August 1
Aug. 8	Aug. 15	Aug. 22	Aug. 30
Sept. 6	Sept. 13	Sept. 21	Sept. 29
Oct. 6	Oct. 13	Oct. 21	Oct. 29
Nov. 4	Nov. 11	Nov. 19	Nov. 27
Dec. 4	Dec. 11	Dec. 19	Dec. 26

Each phase of the Moon lasts approximately seven to eight days, during which the Moon's shape gradually changes as it comes out of one phase and goes into the next.

There will be a solar eclipse during the New Moon phase on June 10 and December 4.

There will be a lunar eclipse during the Full Moon phase on May 26, June 24, and November 19.

Use the Moon phases to connect you with your lucky numbers for this year. See the next page (page 112) and your lucky numbers.

LUCKY NUMBERS
FOR CAPRICORN: 2002

Lucky numbers and astrology can be linked through the movements of the Moon. Each phase of the thirteen Moon cycles vibrates with a sequence of numbers for your Sign of the Zodiac over the course of the year. Using your lucky numbers is a fun system that connects you with tradition.

New Moon	First Quarter	Full Moon	Last Quarter
Dec. 14 ('01)	Dec. 22 ('01)	Dec. 30 ('01)	Jan. 5
1 7 9 0	8 2 7 0	8 4 9 1	1 6 1 0
Jan. 13	Jan. 21	Jan. 28	Feb. 4
1 6 0 6	8 0 4 7	7 3 6 4	4 9 5 2
Feb. 12	Feb. 19	Feb. 27	March 5
7 6 8 2	4 0 7 1	3 8 5 9	3 8 1 9
March 13	March 21	March 28	April 3
2 9 3 6	0 9 3 8	1 9 7 2	1 7 2 2
April 12	April 20	April 26	May 4
3 8 2 9	0 3 9 5	4 8 0 4	3 6 9 9
May 12	May 19	May 26	June 3
4 3 0 6	9 5 7 5	1 6 3 7	7 7 9 2
June 10	June 18	June 24	July 2
6 0 5 8	4 7 5 7	6 3 9 4	4 6 8 0
July 10	July 16	July 24	August 1
0 5 1 4	4 2 7 2	8 3 3 5	5 7 0 4
August 8	August 15	August 22	August 30
6 2 8 8	1 6 2 8	3 7 7 9	3 2 5 4
Sept. 6	Sept. 13	Sept. 21	Sept. 29
8 7 5 0	1 6 3 7	5 8 1 3	6 9 5 8
Oct. 6	Oct. 13	Oct. 21	Oct. 29
2 6 2 7	7 4 8 8	8 1 6 0	5 1 7 7
Nov. 4	Nov. 11	Nov. 19	Nov. 27
9 5 1 7	6 9 3 8	4 6 0 6	6 2 5 3
Dec. 4	Dec. 11	Dec. 19	Dec. 26
5 4 1 5	5 5 7 9	9 3 2 7	1 8 4 9

CAPRICORN
YEARLY FORECAST: 2002

Forecast for 2002 Concerning Business
Prospects, Financial Affairs, Health,
Travel, Employment, Love and Marriage
for Persons Born with the Sun
in the Zodiacal Sign of Capricorn,
December 21–January 19.

This year promises to be a thought-provoking and practical one for those of you born under the influence of the Sun in the zodiacal sign of Capricorn, whose ruler is Saturn, planet of stability and tradition. Family and friends seem to become closer than usual, as you learn to be more expressive with your emotions. Questions of self-improvement are almost bound to lead you toward developing exciting new skills and talents. The business world seems to call for an approach both firm and creative. You will doubtless want to keep an eye on financial developments, and also to make sure rivals are outpaced in the race for customers. Your personal money affairs may look a little unstable from time to time, as your income can fluctuate. However, it's not impossible to work around this and to save useful sums. Your health probably needs some attention, especially if you are working hard and prone to stress. The year 2002 is a promising time to give up unhealthy habits and adopt a better lifestyle. This may be a year that finds you traveling a little less often than usual, but that is not to say that longer trips do not hold out the prospect of pleasure and surprise. It should also be rewarding to explore your own locality in more depth. The prospect for jobs and career concerns suggests that you will not necessarily want to make big changes just yet. What appears more appropriate is to spend time planning your next move, in order to ensure complete success when the time comes. Relationship questions seem to hinge on your own ability to be generous in love. This is a time when you can really begin to develop the kind of deep and supportive partnership that seems close to your ideal.

Since you Capricorns usually are excellent at business matters, you will not be surprised to hear that 2002 will be a promising and successful year. However, there are a couple of areas on which you should keep a beady eye. Finances need to be monitored quite closely, and it is absolutely imperative that you can place full trust in all your employees who deal with company money. During the course of the year, a rival probably will try to poach some of your clients, perhaps by quite underhanded means. You should make sure you keep ahead of the game, maybe by developing new gimmicks that will help ensure customer loyalty. Advertising and publicity can be usefully focused upon sponsorship deals that will keep your company's name in the public eye. Despite the high cost, it may be worthwhile investing in TV advertising as well. Your own role may change as time passes, and an offer of partnership from a former colleague may tempt you to branch out in a new and more lucrative direction. This can indeed be a lucky break for you, but all the same every implication should be carefully weighed before a decision is made. A quiet period during mid-April to the end of May may mean you will have to cut your workforce, perhaps as a temporary measure. This should be dealt with as tactfully as possible in order to keep relations between workers and management sweet. Nor should you work yourself into the ground this year; sometimes increasing success can lead to more responsibility and correspondingly high stress levels. Try not to let your home life be encroached upon. Your instinct for business should serve you well, so you will be able to reach the end of the year with a measure of success tucked under your belt.

Your personal money affairs are likely to fluctuate with changing circumstances, so that periods of affluence are followed by leaner times. The best means of coping with this kind of uncertainty is to put aside funds whenever it is possible to do so, and then you should more readily be able to roll with the punches. If and when you need an extra source of income, there should be no shortage of jobs available, although some of them can be the kind of thing you wouldn't normally think of doing. However, it will not hurt you to try your hand at a new skill to gain a breadth of experience. But do remember that all work and no play will only make you dull. It will not hurt to treat yourself to some really luxurious items when you are in funds. Choose wisely, and buy things that will give lasting pleasure. With some care, you may find yourself slightly better off at the end of the year.

The outlook for health focuses on work-related matters such as tiredness and stress. You Capricorn people can be quite hard on yourselves, but this year is a good time for learning to lighten up a bit. Make sure you factor in a period of relaxation to your daily routine; the difference in the way you feel should be quite dramatic. This will be a very promising time to give up unhealthy habits. You are bound to slip back a few times, but that is all part of the process and can be shrugged off easily. A plainer diet may be in order, especially if you have been relying on junk food rather than cooking proper meals. But don't deny yourself to the extent that eating loses its pleasure. Being too severe with yourself will only make you feel worse rather than better. Finding time for a discipline such as yoga or meditation can make you more aware of the close link between the mind and body, and help you to relax and calm down. The more you can enjoy living a healthier lifestyle, the better chance you have of keeping it up.

Travel to distant places may not seem quite so attractive as usual this year, particularly if your attention is mainly toward other areas of your life. But it can be pleasant to visit friends or relatives who live so far away that you rarely see them; and it would be a treat for them too. Your own locality can yield some pleasant surprises if you make the effort to explore it more thoroughly. It's even possible that you will develop a rewarding interest in local history. Business trips look set for success, although some hard work on negotiations is almost certain to be an essential ingredient for complete satisfaction. It will also help to do some thorough research before you set off; don't rely on the chance of being able to work during the journey. Vacations with an educational flavor may appeal to you at the moment, whether you choose to visit a place that's steeped in history or to take a course during the summer months. This may be the year that youngsters first make the break away from holidaying with the family and go away with their friends. Try to remember that fussing over them will have the opposite effect from what you want to achieve. Your best time for taking a vacation is probably early autumn, between the end of August and mid-October. Aim for a really relaxing time, whatever you are doing. This can ensure happy memories.

Job prospects this year may look somewhat limited at first glance, but there are ways in which you can turn this situation to your advantage. Even though you may not be able to move up the career ladder, this can be an ideal time for planning your future. Money doesn't seem so important at the moment as satisfaction in whatever you are doing. You may even be prepared to take a salary cut, if the job seems right. It will not hurt to capitalize on your natural skills and your sense of duty and responsibility this year; employers will value your input to the full. This can be especially important if you have your eye on getting a good reference. One area that may need some effort on your part is that of relationships within the workplace. Don't be so conscientious that you don't socialize; you will enjoy life far more if you can share a joke with colleagues.

Your main lesson where relationships are concerned seems to be about loosening up emotionally and learning to trust your heart. Impulses of affection shouldn't be stifled, unless the circumstances absolutely forbid it, which isn't often the case. Those of you who are looking for a fresh partner after being single for a while may be forced to choose between two or even more tempting prospects. Do bear in mind that it would be unfair to string someone along without really intending to enter into a serious relationship. Even if you lack confidence in yourself, this is a period when it will probably be brought home to you that love doesn't depend upon good looks or brilliant talents. It is a far more mysterious process that touches everyone's life and is everyone's due. If you have been seeing a special someone for a while now, maybe it's time to start considering real commitment. Nor should you wait for your partner to air this issue if he or she is doing some foot dragging. Being alone isn't necessarily a bad thing at the moment, so those of you who are single should try to relax. You will not be in any doubt when the right person comes along; if you have gained a bit of self-knowledge through being by yourself for a while, it should make the new relationship that much more successful. Whatever your situation, 2002 ought to be a happy year which you will look back on as a time when your relationships became richer and more fulfilling.

CAPRICORN
DAILY FORECAST: 2002

1st Week/January 1–7

Tuesday January 1st. A sense of optimism and hope is likely to pervade the day. Get together with a friend whom you haven't seen in a while and reconnect over lunch. Try to keep your resolutions for the new year realistic and moderate. This will help you to feel successful and motivated when you do accomplish your goals. A phone call tonight can bring cheery news.

Wednesday the 2nd. Love can have a bittersweet quality about it. You may get together with someone attractive, but may also find that there is an obstacle to future romance. Set a limit on how long you will wait for this person, and make sure it is understood. Money can come your way through an investment made a while ago.

Thursday the 3rd. A love interest may have you besotted. Avoid putting the person on a pedestal, however. This will prevent you from being disillusioned later. Cleaning out closets and cupboards can be an industrious way to rid yourself of any excess nervous energy now. Investing in new kitchen utensils and good pots and pans can motivate you to do some cooking.

Friday the 4th. A sharp tongue can get you into some hot water if you aren't careful. Family members and friends may understand your sarcastic humor, but the boss may not. Your patience and discipline can earn you praise when you solve a long-standing problem in the workplace. Apply this same tenacity and get a fabulous workout in at the gym.

Saturday the 5th. People are chatty and sociable, so join a friend for coffee and a walk this morning. Shopping expeditions can yield incredible bargains if you take the time to compare prices. Consider a friend's opinion when deciding on a particular piece of clothing. He or she can have a more objective viewpoint. Pick up some decorating ideas when visiting this evening.

Sunday the 6th. Let a partner take the lead in making current plans. Although you may normally like to be the one in control, you will find that you enjoy yourself immensely. Browse through garage sales and flea markets this afternoon. You can find a treasure or two that would look fabulous in your own home. A female friend may need some advice.

Monday the 7th. This can be a day full of opportunities. Love may be found in a group setting, such as at a meeting of a professional association or in a classroom. An older female friend may come across as rather sarcastic right now. Avoid taking her words to heart. She probably is upset about something that has nothing to do with you.

Weekly Summary

A new business venture looks promising at this time. You should be able to get it off the ground with the right backer. Get the word out to as many people as you can, and someone may come forward quite quickly. In fact, you may attract more than one interested party. You can afford to be choosy about partners.

You may be thinking about taking some courses to expand your knowledge in one particular area at this time. This can be a very smart move on your part. Although it may delay your goal in some respects, it will ensure your success when you do eventually make your move.

You can find yourself in the spotlight in some way right now. Recognition or an award for a job well done is well deserved. A co-worker may be quite jealous of the attention you receive, and can be resentful toward you. Try to be humble so as not to create problems between you. Go out and celebrate with well-wishers.

2nd Week/January 8–15

Tuesday the 8th. Your bank account may be disappearing faster than you would like at this time. Take control of your finances by making a budget that is realistic for your current needs. You can prevent a simple misunderstanding with a family member from escalating into something more by dealing with it now. This should be an auspicious time to be assertive in the workplace as well.

Wednesday the 9th. An urge for freedom and risk taking may overcome you. Don't do anything foolish or adventurous without considering the consequences first. Intuitive and impressionable, you can sense other people's feelings even before they can. You may be quite gullible to other people's suggestions now, so avoid pushy salespeople. In fact, stay away from anyone who doesn't have your best interest at heart.

Thursday the 10th. You may be thrust into the middle of a power play at work. Refuse to participate. It will only backfire on you in the end. Interaction with a dark-haired stranger can be rather intense at this time. There may be something about the person that draws you like a magnet. Realize that your strong feelings may be reciprocated.

Friday the 11th. Hard work seems to be the order of the day. Get up early, and you should accomplish an amazing amount. You work best when left to your own devices right now. Others may just slow you down. Try to arrange a quiet place for yourself, even if it is at home. This evening may best be spent in a low-key manner.

Saturday the 12th. You are at your attractive and charming best today. Someone special may notice you now, and may ask you out. Even if the person does not seem to be your type, give him or her a chance. There may be more there than meets the eye. Listen to some unsolicited financial advice from a savvy older male.

Sunday the 13th. Whatever project you start now will come to a fruitful conclusion within the month. This is a very auspicious time to invest in stocks or bonds, in new business ventures, or in any self-improvement programs. Be sure to consult a professional for any nutritional advice, however. A new haircut should turn out to be fabulous.

Monday the 14th. You are likely to come up with an ingenious new way to make money. Share your scheme with a close friend who may have some expertise that you don't. Together you can make a tidy profit. Schedule in some free time for yourself this afternoon. You can end up feeling trapped and burned out without some downtime.

Weekly Summary

You may be nominated for political office at this time. It can be in local politics, or perhaps just a community board of some kind. Take on the challenge. You can be a powerful motivator and leader right now. Don't let the power go to your head, however. As long as you use your influence with integrity, you can only gain respect.

A long-standing conflict with a family member can now be resolved. It may be so long-standing that you don't even remember what started the standoff. Make a point of initiating contact. Once you sit down and have a heart-to-heart talk, things should fall into place. As you open up, your relative may feel more free to open up as well.

Physical exercise is likely to be more important than usual to your well-being at this time. Consider getting outside and going for a regular walk or hike. The fresh air can do you a world of good mentally and emotionally as well as physically. Another option may be to join a friend and sign up for a class in the martial arts.

3rd Week/January 15–21

Tuesday the 15th. It is more important than usual to be disciplined in all that you do now. This applies especially in any financial dealings. Lucky breaks can come this afternoon when the boss asks you to take on more responsibility. Go for it. You can handle it and receive kudos in the process. Be open to communications with a younger male.

Wednesday the 16th. A delayed project can suddenly take off. Be ready by clearing the decks of all other unfinished business. A get-rich-quick scheme may not be in your best interest right now. Wait for a better option. A close friend may need your time and attention this afternoon. People appreciate your loyalty and caring.

Thursday the 17th. A long-distance venture can look very appealing to you. Don't be afraid to do some more investigation, however. The more you know about it, the more confident you should feel about your decision. Be discerning about recipients of your secrets. Wait until you are with someone whom you know you can trust. Consult an expert for financial success.

Friday the 18th. You may need to put the concerns of a spouse or family member first. This may involve putting some business or personal concerns aside for a while. It probably will be a wise move. Your powers of persuasion seem to be enhanced right now. If you use them when conversing with power players, you can easily win them over to your side.

Saturday the 19th. You may be in the position to expand your circle of friends when you accept an invitation to a party. People you meet there may be very different from your usual crowd. You can make some important contacts. A love relationship can start when a background admirer moves forward. You two should be a great team.

Sunday the 20th. Try to include in your plans your mate, who is quite likely to be feeling left out. A little more care and attention can go a long way toward reigniting some passion between you. Don't get too upset when the car starts acting up. It is probably something very minor. Get it tended to right away, and things should be fine.

Monday the 21st. Your personal image can be especially important to you at this time. Dress for success, and you can impress an important business contact. Shopping expeditions can be very fruitful. Items of quality and luxury will appeal more than bargains. Schedule a massage or manicure while you are at it; you can appreciate these luxuries more than ever.

Weekly Summary

This can be an opportune time to discover your own creative abilities. You seem to have untapped talent in the area of music. If you have ever wanted to sing, this may be the perfect time to sign up for some lessons. Consider joining the local choir, and make some new friends in the process. Learning a new instrument can be another challenge.

It may seem as though you are chauffeuring everyone else in the family around. Maybe you should think about investing in a new vehicle. The extra car can save you time and money in the long run, especially if repair bills are starting to come in on your existing car. Any teenagers in the house will be thrilled by this idea.

Redecorating the house can be done on a budget this week. Although your tastes may be classic and expensive, you can find some great deals at garage sales. Consider changing your environment simply by adding some color. Get some colorful new cushions, and repaint the walls in a new and different shade. You will be amazed at the difference.

4th Week/January 22–28

Tuesday the 22nd. This can be a good day to give that sales pitch that you have been working on. You should be in top form now and can deliver on cue. A romantic attraction can be exciting, but don't expect much to develop. Keep it light and breezy and just have some fun with it. Avoid losing your temper when an older colleague offers some constructive criticism.

Wednesday the 23rd. Your schedule is jammed full at present. Avoid taking on more than you can successfully complete, however. This can prevent you from feeling guilty when you cannot finish everything. A partner may surprise you with a romantic evening tonight. Sit back and let yourself be taken care of for a change.

Thursday the 24th. An office romance may become public. You will feel better once everything is out in the open. Don't be afraid to ask for some expert advice on a financial matter. The more informed you are, the more profit you are likely to make. Take a friend up on an invitation to dinner this evening. Catch up on the news.

Friday the 25th. Don't pretend to agree with a friend if you really do not. Stand up for your own ideas. You will be respected more as a result. Take some time to relax and pamper yourself. You deserve it. Schedule a massage and go out for a gourmet dinner. A partner will be more than happy to come along.

Saturday the 26th. Domestic activities can take up most of the morning. Make plans to spend the rest of the day with the family. Enjoying a sport such as skiing together can put everyone in high spirits. If single, consider inviting a date over for dinner this evening. You can make an impression with your culinary abilities.

Sunday the 27th. It may be time to get back into a regular exercise routine. This can also be a good time to start eating more healthy foods. Enlist the aid of a spouse or other family members. They are likely to be feeling the same way you do, and may want to join in. Tend to any household repairs before they end up costing money.

Monday the 28th. You may find yourself the recipient of praise at work. You will feel that you are finally receiving the recognition that you deserve. An old flame from the past can make an unexpected appearance, wanting to reignite an old relationship. Be very wary. He or she may not have changed as much as you are urged to believe.

Weekly Summary

A job offer can come your way through an association with a particular male friend. It may start at a social event or party. Even if you don't feel like going, it can be in your best interest to attend. Dress your best, and expect to make an important contact. Be aware of whatever possibilities this new job can offer you.

A close friendship may have the possibility of turning into something more. Someone who has been a good friend for a long time can declare romantic feelings for you. Stay receptive to it. Sometimes the best relationships start this way. If you go slow, you two may stand a very good chance of making it work.

An older relative or loved one may be missing your company right now but is too proud to ask for it. A surprise visit will be welcome. Make the person more secure by setting up a consistent day and time to visit. That way there will always be something to look forward to.

5th Week/January 29–February 4

Tuesday the 29th. You can expect to be noted for your astute business sense. An adversary will be duly impressed. He may try to persuade you to join his team. A project should work out better when done with a partner. A female you know well may offer you her services. Together, you can make an unbeatable team. Loyalty can be handsomely rewarded.

Wednesday the 30th. You have a love of luxury and good times which can lead to budgetary bankruptcy if you're not careful. Set a spending limit and stick to it. Better yet, put off large purchases for when you are in a more economical frame of mind. This will be a great night to get friends together for some fun.

Thursday the 31st. Reach for the stars. Once you set your mind to something, nothing is able to stop you. Personal charm and magnetism may be at a high. The urge to go directly for what you want can antagonize someone important. A more indirect route can appease a sensitive ego. You may receive news of a birth.

Friday February 1st. A family member may want to talk about your relationship at this time. You may be accused of being too distant as of late. Think about how to balance home concerns with those of the office. Attention and tender loving care can take care of the problem. Sincerity and humor are your best qualities now.

Saturday the 2nd. You may be in the mood to get rid of unwanted clutter. Clean out of the closets and cupboards. You should feel more emotionally clear as a result. Someone of important social standing may call on you at home. Be ready. An amazing opportunity can be yours as a result. Romance can come from an unexpected source this evening.

Sunday the 3rd. A relationship may be taken to a new level. A commitment of some kind will probably be part of the scenario. Realize that some trepidation is perfectly normal. Beautiful and tranquil surroundings can benefit both mind and body. Consider aesthetic appeal when making plans for this evening. Try the art gallery.

Monday the 4th. You are more likely than usual to focus on love and relationships. A friendship can turn into something more romantic. Curtail a tendency to jump in too quickly, however. Consider long-term effects. Someone fiery and feisty can become an ally. Remind the person that you can fight your own battles. A promise made long ago may be fulfilled.

Weekly Summary

A friend may ask you to become partners in a business venture. Think about it before jumping in too quickly. Your friendship may need to be protected in case things don't work out. Be sure to talk about goals and responsibilities before signing on the dotted line. Once you are both in agreement, you should make a great team.

Thoughts you may have had in the back of your head about taking a trip can now be brought forward. Some time should become available to you in the near future. Take advantage of it, since it may be quite a while before you get another chance. Talk to friends who have been away to get some firsthand knowledge of where you want to go.

A job offer can come to you through a client, who is impressed with your work and may want to hire you.

Don't be too quick to say yes. Be sure to get all the details in writing first. Since loyalty and trust are likely to be very important to you, avoid burning any bridges with your current employer.

6th Week/February 5–11

Tuesday the 5th. You can be of service to someone in need. Your kind act will renew the person's faith in humanity. Clues to a friend's strange behavior may finally fall into place. You can now see more clearly what the problem is. Remind him or her that you can be trusted. A long-lost item can make a sudden appearance.

Wednesday the 6th. Two friends may try to pull you into the middle of a dispute. Do your best to stay out of it. Taking sides would probably not work out well for you. A pet project may take on a life of its own. The time to go public should be getting closer. Just wait a little longer. Trust your intuition.

Thursday the 7th. A power struggle with a female colleague may erupt unexpectedly. Don't back down just to keep the peace. Stand your ground, but be prepared to compromise as well. Your intuition can be a source of inspiration for a creative project. Spend some quiet time alone and tap into it. Bounce your ideas off a trusted friend.

Friday the 8th. Lady Luck will be on your side. Don't be afraid to ask directly for what you want now; you are very likely to get it. This can be a great day to ask the boss for a raise or to ask important people for important favors. Avoid any inclination toward becoming too self-centered, however. Develop a give-and-take attitude.

Saturday the 9th. At this time you tell it like it is. Remember to temper your honesty with tact, however. This can enable others to better hear your message. You may be feeling a strong sense of responsibility toward siblings or relatives right now. Realize that they may need to stand on their own two feet at this time. Give them space.

Sunday the 10th. A love relationship may hit a snag. It is likely either to end or to go to a new level. It will probably be up to you how much energy you want to invest in it. Time spent with a close friend can be a great way to while away the afternoon.

Monday the 11th. Whatever you start now will probably come to a successful conclusion within the month. This should be an auspicious time to start new projects and to break away from old habits and routines. Dare to be different. A conversation with an attractive stranger can leave you wanting more. You may get a yes if you ask for a date.

Weekly Summary

You may be having second thoughts about old friends when something they do hurts your feelings. You may feel a sense of loyalty toward them simply because they have been in your life for so long. They may no longer have your best interests at heart, however. Have a talk with them and decide if it is time to cut the cord.

You may be feeling slightly burned out from the hectic workweek. Instead of pushing yourself to do more, take some time out to recuperate. Pushing yourself forward can deplete your energy reserves even more, and you can make some unnecessary mistakes. A day or two of rest can make all the difference in how you feel and in your work performance.

A male relative may be pushing your buttons. He can be trying to manipulate you into doing something that he wants you to do. Don't buy into his guilt trip. Tell him that he needs to be responsible for himself. His respect for you should grow as a result.

7th Week/February 12–18

Tuesday the 12th. You are blessed with the ability to attract money to you. This is a great time to get involved in a new business or financial venture. Females tend to be lucky for you at this time. Be sure to interact with them as much as possible now. An older woman can have some savvy advice.

Wednesday the 13th. Expect the unexpected. Keep plans flexible just in case. If a project is not going the way that you would like, refrain from throwing the whole thing out and starting again. You should be able to save it with a few minor adjustments. Enlist the aid of an objective friend. Patience will be your keyword.

Thursday the 14th. You will be out and around a fair bit running errands. People will be in a chatty mood, so be prepared to stop and talk while on your travels. Someone you meet on the coffee line can prove to be a fascinating conversationalist. You may find yourself thinking about a new romance on this Valentine's Day.

Friday the 15th. You may be in a more impatient mood than usual. You want to get things done quickly. Try to leave the more ponderous and detail-oriented tasks for another day. You should excel at physical activities now. Work up a sweat at the gym, or roll up your sleeves and clean the house from top to bottom.

Saturday the 16th. You find that your energy levels are very high. You attack tasks with enthusiasm and zeal. You may find yourself in the company of men, one of whom in particular can end up being a mentor to you in some way. It may not be so much what he says, but what he does that inspires you. Some interesting news can come your way.

Sunday the 17th. Interactions with others will be more intense than usual. You can get to the core of a conflict with a friend and resolve it for good. Older relatives may be coming across as somewhat sentimental right now. Flip through old photo albums with them and listen to their stories about the good old days.

Monday the 18th. Responsibility is your current keyword. You probably will not be able to take a shortcut on anything, so don't even bother trying. If you haven't been paying attention to finances, you may find that you are refused a credit card. A love relationship can move to a new level if you both sit down and have a heart-to-heart talk.

Weekly Summary

You are more likely than usual to feel an urge toward nurturing this week. If you have kids, you probably will be spending a lot of time with them. If you don't, think of other ways to fulfill this need. Planting flowers and herbs and tending to them as they grow can bring contentment. Getting a pet can be another good idea.

Your communication skills may be enhanced. You should be able to impress colleagues during a verbal presentation. Say yes if you are invited to participate in a debate. Although it may seem threatening at first, you have the ability to think on your feet now. You may even find that you excel under pressure.

This will be an opportune time to invite the boss over for dinner. He may be more prone than usual to being impressed with your efforts. Be sure to do the cooking yourself to win even more points. Once the boss sees you in this new light, he will think even more highly of you than before.

8th Week/February 19–25

Tuesday the 19th. You are really enjoying the physical pleasures of life now. Schedule a massage or facial and relax. Good food, good wine, and good company are what will make you happy this evening, so arrange it early in the day. A shopping trip can yield some good bargains, but it can be easy to give in to temptation and overspend.

Wednesday the 20th. Get any dentist's or doctor's visits over with now if you have been putting them off. Make a trip to the health food store and stock up on all your vitamins and health supplements. You may find that you want more intellectual stimulation, so browse through a night school course catalogue and see what strikes your fancy.

Thursday the 21st. You are in the mood to speak your mind, but be careful when it comes to giving advice. One friend in particular may not understand that you are just trying to help. You can have an ear for language now. Accents seem to roll off your tongue fairly easily at this time.

Friday the 22nd. There is a lot of electricity in the air, and you can probably feel it. Try to use this energy for constructive activities. If you don't consciously channel it, you can find yourself becoming irritated by little annoyances. Activities that require speed and efficiency are supported. A woman from your past may call with some amazing news.

Saturday the 23rd. A friend may want you to pin down plans. Although you may not feel like committing yourself, you can lose out if you don't. Your mind sees things more logically and rationally than usual. Try to stay in tune with your emotions as well, however. They can help you to answer a question of the heart.

Sunday the 24th. This can be a very auspicious day for new beginnings. Whatever you do now should come to a successful conclusion. It can be a great day for getting married, opening a new business, or going on a first date. Large ticket purchases bought now will prove to be of lasting value. Clothes bought now can turn out to be favorites.

Monday the 25th. It may be time to think about changing financial institutions. The one you are currently dealing with may not be giving you the very best rates for your investments. Ask friends and shop around. You can do better. You may be thrust unexpectedly into the spotlight at work now. Be ready with all the facts if asked to give an impromptu presentation.

Weekly Summary

Spending time with children can be very fulfilling. If you have kids of your own, be sure to take some quality time off by yourselves. If you don't have kids, ask to borrow your nieces and nephews for a while. The neighbors will be thrilled if you offer to baby-sit for free one night. Get your fill, and then give them back.

You may be thinking about how to work more physical fitness into your daily routine. You may actually have to schedule it in. You are someone who does better in the mornings, so consider getting it in before work. If not, ask a spouse or close friend to meet you in the evenings. That way, you are less likely to skip it.

You may be investing a lot of your time and energy in a brand-new romance right now. Although the first stages of love are grand, do your best to concentrate on your own life too. Too much togetherness too fast can lead to early burnout. Maintain a slight distance for a while.

9th Week/February 26–March 4

Tuesday the 26th. Your emotions tend to be quite volatile, especially in a love relationship. If a love interest asks for more space, give it. The person will return soon enough. This may be a test of your faith and of your self-respect. Take on the challenge. You can make money from investments dealing with power sources.

Wednesday the 27th. You probably are setting a very high standard of performance for yourself. You can waste valuable time and energy trying to be perfect, however, so know when good enough is good enough. You have a good eye for detail now. Use this skill to balance your bank book, take up needlepoint, or paint something beautiful.

Thursday the 28th. Travel could be on your mind. If you cannot take the time for an extended holiday, try to get away for a few days. You should return with a broadened perspective on things. The kids may be clamoring for a new pet. This can be a good time to bring one home. Visit the local animal shelter and surprise the family.

Friday March 1st. Career issues may be on your mind. Try to concentrate more on your long-range goals right now. With these in mind, it will be easier to make short-term decisions. The boss may be acting more friendly than usual. It may not be the best time to ask for a raise, however.

Saturday the 2nd. Tonight will be a very auspicious time to throw a party. Although last-minute, people should be quite happy to accept your invitation. If you cannot give a party, attend one. Someone you meet tonight will have an important effect on your future, either romantically or financially. Keep your eyes open for someone fair, charming, and intelligent.

Sunday the 3rd. You may be thrust into the middle of other people's problems this morning. Play the peace-maker for a while, but know when to call it quits. Sometimes people just don't want help from others. A partner can be acting unusually jealous. Realize that some reassurance of your feelings is needed. Give it immediately.

Monday the 4th. Love can be like a roller coaster ride. Expect the unexpected. If things take a turn for the worse, ride it out, knowing that they are just as likely to turn around again. A female friend may be very vague about what she needs from you right now. Talking to her for a while can help her to get more clear.

Weekly Summary

You can be thinking about your long-term financial security this week. Conservative investments will work to your benefit. Enlist the aid of a financial expert before making any commitments in writing. Pooling your resources with those of a partner, relative, or sibling can enable you to reap even greater benefits. Get clear on your mutual goals first.

Your dream vacation may now seem like a reality. You can be given the green light to take time away from work. Planning your trip can be almost as much fun as taking it. Go to the library and research exactly where you want to go. If going alone, expect to meet someone special en route. You may end up sightseeing together.

Your executive ability is showing through right about now. A challenging project at work may have called upon you to use your skills of organization and leadership. Higher-ups will be duly impressed, and may offer to promote you. Make sure that the promotion comes with a commensurate raise in pay, however.

10th Week/March 5–11

Tuesday the 5th. Your way is the direct way now. Forthright in speech and manner, you are sure to get your point across. Do watch a tendency to be too blunt, however. Others may appreciate candor, but not insensitivity. Insightful ideas can come to you at a fast and furious pace, but it may be best to censor them before presenting them.

Wednesday the 6th. A conservative attitude should prevail where money is concerned. It will be easier than usual to stick to the budget now. You can get a good deal on a major purchase. A younger friend's elusive attitude may compel you to dig deeper for answers. Be forewarned. You may end up learning much more than you bargained for.

Thursday the 7th. You can attract an admirer at a social event this evening. This dark and mysterious stranger will captivate you as well. You may have something in common, so you may feel like you have found a kindred spirit. A new facet of your work may become apparent. Think about ways to pursue and benefit from this realization.

Friday the 8th. You now can assimilate facts and details better than usual. This can be a great time to learn a new language or to take a course in something that interests you. A rebellious attitude may rub a co-worker the wrong way. Use tact and diplomacy when expressing strong opinions. You can still get your point across clearly.

Saturday the 9th. You may be thrust into the spotlight at a group function. Be sure to state your point of view with confidence; someone important to your future may be listening. You are happy to know that you are making a good impression. Don't discard a plan that doesn't work out well right now. It may still be a good idea. Remember that timing can be everything.

Sunday the 10th. Your intuition is probably on the mark, and it can help you to see the bigger picture. Other people's motivations may become more apparent. You are extra sensitive now, both physically and emotionally. Be careful whom you allow into your space. A healthy diet can keep a sensitive stomach happy, so you will be happy too.

Monday the 11th. Take the time to contemplate an important decision. Your exuberant enthusiasm can cause you to overlook details. A talk with a trusted friend can help you to see all the angles. You may be asked to lend a hand to a charity or service organization. The camaraderie you feel will make it worth all the effort.

Weekly Summary

You may be called upon to make a speech to a large audience. Although you may be given ample time to prepare, you still can be tentative. Realize that it may be quite normal to be afraid of public speaking. The best thing for you to do is to practice. Rest assured that your eloquence can win over any audience.

It is more important than usual for you to spend some time on your own. If this is not something that you do normally, it will be all the more important. If you cannot take the time off, at least plan for a free afternoon. Go off somewhere by yourself, preferably into nature where it's quiet. You may be amazed at what you hear when you tune in.

You will be more self-assertive than usual this week. It should be okay to put yourself forward now, as others will make room for you. This can be an auspicious time to go public with a bold new venture. Publish a new book, display artwork, or start advertising campaigns.

11th Week/March 12–18

Tuesday the 12th. A new moneymaking idea can come to you out of the blue. Don't dismiss it as fantasy right away. There may be elements of it that are quite practical. You may be feeling a strong sense of compassion for people in need. Show them how much you care about their welfare. Their appreciation will be apparent.

Wednesday the 13th. Whatever you start is likely to come to a fruitful conclusion within the month. You tend to be especially favored in artistic, spiritual, and creative projects at this time. Doing anything that inspires you or touches the heart can work out to your advantage. But be sure to keep an eye on the budget as well.

Thursday the 14th. You may be out and around a lot more than usual. Catch up on correspondence and run errands. Expect the phone to be ringing off the hook now. A minor dispute with neighbors can be resolved with a little tact and diplomacy on your part. Once they have your attention, they are likely to listen to your point of view.

Friday the 15th. People in the world may seem to be moving a little faster than usual. You may be feeling a little impatient yourself right now. Bite your tongue before losing your temper with a loved one. You can channel this energy successfully through physical exercise or work. Roll up your sleeves and rearrange the office or living room.

Saturday the 16th. You may have a tendency to rush headlong into love. You can feel an instant and intense attraction to someone you meet in a social arena. The attraction can be mutual. Enjoy this heady feeling, but try to keep your wits about you as well. Remember that you probably don't know everything about the person yet.

Sunday the 17th. Action is your keyword this weekend. Get out there and keep moving. Tend to some yard work, or join a friend for a hike in the woods. Avoid becoming impatient in traffic, however. The police are not likely to just give warnings at this time. A mate can become stubborn if pushed too hard.

Monday the 18th. You can expect to be very consistent in your work efforts. Disciplined and focused, you will get the job done. The boss may see you as someone to be counted on, and say so. Miscommunications can be part of the scenario now, so be sure to choose your words carefully. Do things requiring logic.

Weekly Summary

It will be to your benefit to make up a monthly budget. Realize that this can help you to achieve your financial goals more quickly. Although tedious, it can make you more aware of how much you actually spend. Avoid becoming too stringent in your zeal to save money. Allow yourself the occasional indulgence to keep yourself happy.

Interactions with a sibling can be unusually strained right now. Perhaps there is a long-standing resentment that has been triggered once again. This can be the time to resolve things for good. It may be up to you to initiate a discussion, however. Make a point of just listening for a while. Defenses should go down, and headway can then be made.

You may find yourself feeling overprotective of children right now. Although normal, it may be in their best interest to back off a little bit. They probably need more room to make their own mistakes right now. Don't forget that they are likely to learn more this way.

12th Week/March 19–25

Tuesday the 19th. Creative expression is high on your list of priorities. Go to a paint-it-yourself ceramic place and create your own beautiful mug or colorful plate. You will have an incredible feeling of satisfaction every time you drink coffee from that mug. Good food and good company can bring you pleasure this evening when an intellectually stimulating friend joins you for dinner.

Wednesday the 20th. You can excel in all manner of craftsmanship. You probably will not turn in a project unless it is just perfect. You may be asked to show a new colleague the ropes. Be extra nice about it, as the person can be a valuable ally to you in the future. A younger friend will keep you laughing this evening.

Thursday the 21st. An old friend may come back into your life. If this person was a romantic partner, be very wary of starting the romance over again. You are more quick-witted than usual now and can keep conversations alive with your wry sense of humor. You may be very popular, so expect to be invited to more than one social event.

Friday the 22nd. A partner may complain that you aren't spending enough time at home. Appease the concern by making plans for just the two of you this weekend. Attend to household matters. Have a quiet time at home together this evening. Cook a nice dinner, and then rent a romantic video. All should be calm on the relationship front as a result.

Saturday the 23rd. You are more emotionally sensitive than usual. A friend can inadvertently hurt your feelings when trying to be funny. Don't take it to heart. This can be a great evening to invite friends over for a get-together. If cooking isn't your thing, organize a pot-luck dinner. With everyone pitching in, you can relax and have fun yourself.

Sunday the 24th. Your heart is in agreement with your head when making an important decision. You should know that you are on the right track. Children may be more demanding than usual right now. Give them the attention that they may be craving, and you should notice a calming change in their attitude.

Monday the 25th. Investing with a partner can reap larger profits for you in the long run. Consider pooling your resources with a loved one. Just be sure to be clear about your mutual goals. Attend the opera or a musical performance this evening. You appreciate grand theater most at this time. Dress to the nines while you're at it.

Weekly Summary

You are most likely to seek glamour and fantasy in your life right now. Wining and dining may be high on your list of priorities. Indulge your craving, and set up the perfect romantic evening. Include candlelight and long, lingering looks. If committed, your partner will be enchanted. If single, your date will be swept off his or her feet.

It may be time now to get back to a regular daily routine. You may have been sidetracked by unexpected time constraints due to work and have skipped your usual rituals. Now you realize that these rituals are more important than previously thought. Take some time for yourself every morning to read the paper and have your coffee without interruptions.

You are more appreciative of the beauty in all things right now. This appreciation can extend to people as well. Avoid taking second looks at others when with your partner, who may not take kindly to your resurgence of aesthetic appreciation. Appreciate the beauty in your mate as well, and be sure to verbalize it.

13th Week/March 26–April 1

Tuesday the 26th. You can be supported in going public with your plans. After all your planning and hard work, it is time to present the final product. Consider investing in professional publicity. This can help to reach a wider audience. A younger male can be jealous of your accomplishments. Avoid gloating, even though his attitude may make you want to rub it in.

Wednesday the 27th. Avoid taking on more than you can handle. Optimistic and enthusiastic, you are quite likely to overextend yourself. Bounce your ideas off of a pragmatic and practical friend who can help to keep you grounded in reality. Be sure to count your change at the grocery store cashier. You can get shortchanged if you aren't paying attention.

Thursday the 28th. People expect others to be very courteous now, so mind your manners. A meeting with the boss may have you a little nervous. Relax. He probably just wants to tell you what a good job you have been doing. Relationships of all kinds run quite smoothly now if you are lighting a Passover candle; loved ones will make the ceremony even brighter.

Friday the 29th. You may react strongly to injustices. Be careful when standing up for someone else right now. You may be getting involved in more than you bargained for. Consider writing an editorial to the local paper, expressing your views about something that bothers you. You will have a good chance of being published.

Saturday the 30th. Your mind this weekend may be focused on finances, or lack of them. Money may be flowing out more quickly than it's coming in. You seem to have a talent for making old things new again, so consider browsing through garage sales and refurbishing old pieces of furniture to sell. You can make a bundle.

Sunday the 31st. You may be feeling slightly insecure and unfocused this Easter Sunday. Realize that you may be reassessing your future goals and priorities, and still are unsure of where to go. Stop worrying. Enjoy a family dinner. The answer should come later after you have spent some time alone. Get outdoors. A hike in the woods can help you to refocus.

Monday April 1st. You will be in an optimistic mood. Others find your enthusiasm to be contagious and may gravitate toward you as a result. Humor can alleviate a stressful situation with a colleague. Once you get people laughing, they will be much easier to get along with. Have fun playing games this evening. Get out the chess or checkerboard.

Weekly Summary

You may be thinking about launching into a new business venture this week. Finding financing can be holding you back. Although going into debt can be scary, it may be worth the risk. If you don't want to make a bank loan, there may be someone quite close to you who would like to be part of your venture. A close family friend may be interested.

You probably are thinking of your life in more philosophical terms right now. A conversation with someone very wise can open an expanded vision of your life. Consider taking a trip to a different culture. Their customs can help to broaden your perspective on life.

You are likely to balk at authority now, which can make it difficult to take orders from the boss. Try to work as independently as possible at this time. Immerse yourself in projects that allow you to take the lead or to be in command. Once the boss sees how self-reliant you are, you will get more leeway to do your own thing.

14th Week/April 2–8

Tuesday the 2nd. Don't take the words of an acquaintance at face value. Probably there is something that you are not being told. Dig deeper to find the facts. A controlling female may try to shame you into doing something that benefits her. Don't fall for her manipulative tactics. Resolve to avoid this person in the future if possible.

Wednesday the 3rd. Things have a good chance of going your way. Don't be afraid to be direct and to ask for what you want. A professional male can be impressed by your assertive and confident attitude right now. Expect to be offered a job. Dare to take a chance. Whatever you do now should work out to your benefit.

Thursday the 4th. Your efforts in the workplace will be recognized in some form. You may receive a commendation or even a promotion or raise. A miscommunication with a relative can be cleared up if you deal with it immediately. This will prevent it from escalating into something bigger. You never know whom you will bump into, so dress your best.

Friday the 5th. Romantic relationships probably will take most of your attention. If single, you are bound to meet someone interesting and attractive at a social function connected to your work. This person will be dark, humorous, and successful. Together you can make an unbeatable team professionally as well as romantically. Check it out.

Saturday the 6th. A friend may try to recruit you to be part of a humanitarian cause. Consider joining the team. Your business and organizational skills can really make a difference to any such efforts. A close friend may cancel on you at the last minute this evening. Don't just stay home. Someone else will be glad to go out with you.

Sunday the 7th. People seem to want to talk more than usual. You may be quite chatty yourself. You are inclined to analyze things intellectually right now, including emotions. Try to maintain a balance between your head and your heart. Writers and speakers may need to get out of their own way and allow the words just to flow.

Monday the 8th. Try not to think too far ahead because it can prevent you from living in and enjoying the present moment. Be receptive and ready when opportunity knocks on your door. It will change your life if you decide to take advantage of it. Money may come your way in the form of repayment of an old debt.

Weekly Summary

You may want to expand your circle of friends at this time. Perhaps you are changing on an emotional or mental level and want to meet people who are more congenial. Sign up for a class that interests you. Someone that you meet there can become a very close friend indeed. You should share some very intellectually stimulating conversations.

Your intuition will be right on target this week. You may be prone to dismiss it, choosing instead to rationalize things. Try a little experiment. Whenever your intuition tells you to do something, do it just to see what the outcome is. After a while, you may be amazed at how accurate your timing can be.

You may come across as quite assertive at this time. Asking for what you want can be very empowering, but make sure that you are respectful of others as well.

There is a fine line between assertion and aggression. Aggression can only backfire on you. Know when to back off.

15th Week/April 9–15

Tuesday the 9th. You may be eager to put a domestic plan into action, but it may depend upon the support of other family members. State your case clearly, and you should receive the support you desire. Shopping may be a favorite pastime, but be sure to pay for any expensive items with cash instead of credit for the time being.

Wednesday the 10th. You may be more psychic than usual now, and can pick up on the feelings of others. A friend in need may appreciate your compassion and sensitivity to his or her feelings. You may have very dramatic and prophetic dreams at this time. Consider writing them down to see what messages are there for you.

Thursday the 11th. You will feel good about a financial opportunity that comes your way. It can mean taking a few risks; but as long as you don't go to extremes, it should all work out to your advantage. Be sure that your information comes from a reliable source, however. Agree to disagree with a colleague.

Friday the 12th. Close friends may confide in you. Recognizing their complete and utter trust in you should help to bring you even closer. Don't let a family member's attitude affect your good mood. You do not really have anything to feel guilty about. A defensive child may need to be listened to more, so sit back and let him or her talk.

Saturday the 13th. Get household chores and tasks accomplished early in the day. This allows you to move on to something more fun and rewarding this afternoon. You may think people are talking behind your back right now. Avoid becoming paranoid. If they are, it may well be a compliment to you. Lose yourself in a creative hobby this afternoon.

Sunday the 14th. Although you try to avoid confrontations, you may need to address a situation head-on. A relative may be acting in a way that you find very disrespectful. Address it now and move on; the person will not mess with you again. Try to see things from a partner's point of view this evening. Sit back and let the other take the lead.

Monday the 15th. There is a strong possibility that you will be feeling dreamy and introspective. Delegate any work that you don't feel up to doing right now. Be sure to get away for some time on your own. This can be an incredibly creative time, and inspiration can come when you tune in. Lose yourself in a good book or movie this evening.

Weekly Summary

You have an appreciation for the finer things in life right now. If you are thinking of buying fine wine or beautiful jewelry, consider them an investment. A beautiful piece of artwork can also be considered an investment, but you get to hang it in your living room and appreciate it every day.

This can be an opportune time to buy electronic or technological equipment. Consider upgrading your current computer system. You can find a great deal if you search for bargains. Talk to friends to see what works for them. A new sound or stereo system may be part of the scenario. Be sure to get a warranty, however. You may want to upgrade more quickly than you anticipate.

This can be a very good time to tend to any household repairs that you have been putting off. Check the insulation in the roof and the walls. You may be able to save even more money in the long run if you replace it completely. Kitchen appliances may need to be replaced, but be sure to check the warranty beforehand.

16th Week/April 16–22

Tuesday the 16th. Be aware of unspoken messages, and read between the lines. Someone may be trying to make a point but may not have the courage to be direct about it. You have a lot of self-discipline right now and can stick to any diet plans or health routines. This can be a good time to invest in new exercise equipment.

Wednesday the 17th. An important financial opportunity may come to your attention. Don't let it pass you by. Although you initially react in a conservative manner, this may be a good time to take a small risk. If you are too antsy to work behind a desk right now, try to get outside and get some exercise. Your mental outlook should improve as well.

Thursday the 18th. Organization will be your keyword now. You will amaze even yourself with the amount of work that you are able to accomplish. You may be surprised to receive a phone call from someone from your distant past, who is likely to be wanting something from you. Reserve judgment until you know what it is.

Friday the 19th. Relationships with business partners and colleagues run more smoothly than usual. Put your heads together and make some plans for your future.

Nothing can stop you once you reach agreement on your mutual goals. If single, you may meet the partner of your dreams this evening at an informal get-together. Be sure to dress your best.

Saturday the 20th. You will be considering ending a friendship at this time. Perhaps an old friend has given you a promise, then let you down at the last minute. Protect yourself from this ever happening again by ending the association. Let your hair down and go out on the town this evening. You deserve to have a little fun.

Sunday the 21st. Make an extra effort to hold on to your temper. Little things irritate you now. Physical exercise can be a good way to burn off any nervous energy and help to calm you down. Watch your driving right now, as speed traps are numerous. Put off any shopping expeditions for another time when you're not so impulsive.

Monday the 22nd. You are in the mood for hard work, and woe betide anyone around you who isn't. Others will be motivated when they see you in action. An older male relative may come across as patronizing when he offers you some unsolicited career advice. Avoid becoming defensive. Just thank him for his concern and let it go.

Weekly Summary

You may be in the mood to enjoy the best of what life has to offer this week. Even if the budget is strained, you can probably rationalize an evening out. Go out for a lavish dinner with a loved one. Good wine and good company make life worth living. Realize that you may need to be rewarded after all your hard work lately.

Cleaning and organizing are high on your list of priorities right now. Roll up your sleeves and clean out closets and cupboards. Weed out any old clothes and take them to the secondhand clothing store. You might as well make some money while you're at it. A sense of calmness and satisfaction should be the result of all this effort.

You may be considering the idea of going into business with a close friend. You may need to talk about things a fair bit before you make any final decisions. Figure out a way to protect your friendship in case the business doesn't work out. Once you get things clear, you can do well in a partnership.

17th Week/April 23–29

Tuesday the 23rd. Your work ethic seems to be quite stringent. You may be your own worst critic. Lighten up. Believe colleagues when they compliment you on a job well done. Tend to a minor health concern now. This can prevent you from doing unnecessary worrying. If a pet is acting up, it may be because it needs more of your attention.

Wednesday the 24th. Issues of commitment can arise in a love relationship. It will be futile to try to pressure another into making things more serious. If he or she is not ready, decide whether you really are willing to wait around. Money can be made from unorthodox means. You may be seen as brilliant for coming up with this idea.

Thursday the 25th. Cooperation with others will be easier than usual. A spouse or love interest may come up with an idea of how you two can go into business together. This can be a very feasible option that may bring you even closer together. You want beauty in your environment. Pick up some flowers on your way home tonight.

Friday the 26th. Since the boss seems to be more approachable than usual, this can be an auspicious time to ask for a raise. You may find yourself in the company of women, one of whom in particular has some very astute financial advice for you. Listen to her. A phone call from a distant land can bring happy news tonight.

Saturday the 27th. Refuse to react if a love interest tries to make you jealous. Realize that this ploy is a matter of insecurity. Resolve to reassure your love of your feelings on a more consistent basis. You may be playing detective when a valuable item goes missing. Check places that are dark and low, as it could have fallen behind something.

Sunday the 28th. You should have tremendous discipline and self-control. It will be easier than usual to stick to any new dietary or health regimens. Avoid becoming stubborn, however. Stay flexible when discussing vacation plans with a mate. Putting your foot down can result only in defensiveness on both of your parts. Stay receptive to new and different ideas.

Monday the 29th. You will start the day off in high spirits. Tackle work early and you should get much accomplished. Your energy may wane as the day wears on, however. Consider packing it in early and get home to spend some quality time with the kids. Physical activity can help you to reenergize. Try to get outside for some fresh air.

Weekly Summary

You seem to have incredibly focused and intense mental powers this week. Once you start something, you probably will not stop until you are finished. This lends itself well to any kind of investigative work. Researchers should find the information that they are looking for. This kind of passion can translate into your love life as well.

Some of you may be involved in some kind of legal procedure. As long as you tell the whole truth, things will work out in your favor. Holding back even the smallest piece of information can hurt your case. Don't fall for any scare tactics from the opposing side. This kind of manipulation may only show that they are worried.

Older relatives may be complaining that they don't see enough of you. Consider setting up a regularly scheduled visit. If they know when they can count on seeing you, they are less likely to worry. This kind of consistency can help them to feel loved and cared about. Spend some time doing things that they like, such as browsing through old photo albums.

18th Week/April 30–May 6

Tuesday the 30th. A love from the past may make a sudden appearance. This can be your chance to resolve some old issues between the two of you. It may be possible to salvage a friendship out of this whole situation. Watch your speech at this time. You may think you're being funny, but a more sensitive friend may not share your sentiments.

Wednesday May 1st. Things are working out in your favor. This can be a good time to ask someone for a date or to apply for a new job. Others make room for you now. Your executive ability may show itself when you take over in a crisis at work. The boss is sure to be suitably impressed.

Thursday the 2nd. You can be looking at the world through rose-colored glasses. Enjoy the experience, but avoid being gullible where business is concerned. Put off any important decisions for a time when you are more focused. This should be a fine time for romance, however. Dining with candlelight, roses, and someone special should fill the bill for this evening.

Friday the 3rd. Remain strong in the face of fierce opposition. Your faith in yourself and your plan may be being tested. Calm resolve is what can win for you now. Others will back off when they sense your unruffled conviction. Putting off making a particular phone call may only make it harder. All will turn out well in the end.

Saturday the 4th. Love and luck can go hand-in-hand this weekend. You can find one while pursuing the other. Money matters may be looking up. A financial opportunity found through a loved one bears looking into. You may be in the spotlight now. Accept the acclaim graciously. Time spent outdoors can rejuvenate the soul.

Sunday the 5th. A romantic partner may make an unexpected proposition. Consider it carefully before dismissing it out of hand. Trying something new together can only strengthen your relationship. You may learn to trust each other more as a result. The successful outcome of a project can have even you surprised. Confidence in yourself will be renewed.

Monday the 6th. A female friend is puzzling you. The direct approach may only distance her more, however. Subtlety and tact in conversation can help you to understand her motives. She will appreciate you as an understanding and sensitive friend as a result. Love possibilities are likely to abound everywhere. You may even find one right next door.

Weekly Summary

You can be feeling a stronger sense of compassion for your fellowmen right now. Consider volunteering some time to a humanitarian organization or charity. Lend it your talents of organization and leadership. With you on its side, it is bound to make considerable headway. You can also do well on a social committee organizing fund-raisers.

You probably will react more negatively than usual to confinement of any kind. You need a lot of room to move right now. Try to get outside into nature as much as you can. Making commitments of any kind can be very difficult. This can be a good time just to take off on a holiday with no agenda or itinerary.

A little selfishness can be considered a good thing right now. You may have been so caught up in the problems of others lately that you have neglected yourself. Learn to set boundaries and to say no sometimes when people ask you favors. Remember that if you are burned-out, you cannot be good for anybody, let alone yourself.

19th Week/May 7–13

Tuesday the 7th. You can find a way to incorporate new ideas into old routines. Daily tasks and habits can be restructured into a more efficient regime. Pay attention to details now. The person in charge may want to see all the supportive documentation. Be aware of this when applying for a loan or simply asking someone for a favor.

Wednesday the 8th. The world of romantic fantasy can be enticing. You appreciate beauty now. Attempts made to make yourself as attractive as possible will be met with approval. Your heightened sensitivity can allow you to indulge in sensual pleasures. Allow yourself to escape from the real world for a while. Enjoy a good book or movie.

Thursday the 9th. Your independent action will be respected. You may need to take a stand apart from others now. Speaking the truth is favored. This kind of integrity may be noticed by higher-ups. Watch a tendency toward bluntness in speech, however. You may think that you're being witty, but others may see it as sarcasm.

Friday the 10th. Duty may call, and a romantic interest will not be too happy about it. Promises of a future getaway together can help to smooth the waters. Employing innovative techniques can allow you to finish up responsibilities early. Take some time for yourself this afternoon. Allow everyone else's demands to fall away for once.

Saturday the 11th. A younger colleague may impart some important information to you. You can be asked to keep it quiet for a while. Use this information carefully. You may need to check up on the facts before completely trusting it, however. A financial boon may be coming your way. It can involve cooperation with another person.

Sunday the 12th. Your future financial security may be paramount in your mind. Long-term investment choices can help to bring you peace of mind. Now is a great time to make a grand plan for your future. Take into consideration advice from someone in the know. Shop for bargains in unusual places. You may uncover something special.

Monday the 13th. A sudden announcement can take you by surprise. A trusted friend may have some news for you. Take it in stride. Resistance can only make it harder to assimilate. You may find that you eventually like what comes from the situation. Avoid arguing with a loved one tonight, even if you feel strongly about your position.

Weekly Summary

Consider hiring a professional to go over your investment portfolio and budget with you. Although you probably have things under control, you may get some valuable new information that will increase your profit margin. Think about setting up a semiannual appointment just to keep yourself abreast of new developments. You may also learn a few tricks of the trade.

New neighbors may be moving in next door. Go out of your way to make them feel welcome. They may become valuable allies to you in the future. You may find that you actually have a lot in common once you get to know each other. If both families have kids, you may see each other as built-in baby-sitters.

You can be considering investing in real estate at this time, which can be a very smart move on your part. You may find just the right house, although it may be slightly out of your price range. Consider going for it anyway. The profit that you make in the long run can make the financial stretch worthwhile. Make an offer.

20th Week/May 14–20

Tuesday the 14th. Your magnetism and charisma will be at a peak. Witty and charming, you should attract a host of admirers. You can afford to be choosy right now, so don't settle for the first one that comes along. Communication seems to be your forte at present. You can hold the audience in the palm of your hand during any verbal presentations.

Wednesday the 15th. You may want to spend the day around the house. Domestic activities can bring more satisfaction than usual at this time. Concoct some new gourmet delight. The family will gladly offer to taste-test for you. Be very careful of the emotions of children. They may need some extra reassurance and support from you.

Thursday the 16th. Avoid putting loved ones up on a pedestal. You may think that they can do no wrong, but they are only human after all. Try to see them in a more realistic light to prevent disappointment later on. Artists and writers are more likely than usual to find divine inspiration. Tackle a creative project this afternoon.

Friday the 17th. You may find yourself attracted to someone who seems larger than life. Don't be fooled by social exterior. The person may be quite insecure on the inside. Reserve judgment until you know him or her better. Spend some time on yourself now. You may be due for an image update. Invest in some new clothes or a haircut that better expresses the real you.

Saturday the 18th. A female friend may seem more distant than usual. Don't assume that it is because of something that you did. You may have to confront her directly to get at the truth. Tonight may have been made for romance, so go out on the town. A little dining, dancing, and candlelight with a loved one can set the mood perfectly.

Sunday the 19th. You can feel an urge to get away for the day. Take a little road trip and do some sightseeing. Traveling can help you to put any problems into their proper perspective. You may have been blowing them out of proportion. A male relative may have some surprising news this evening. Gather the family together and celebrate.

Monday the 20th. You will have an enhanced need for order in your environment. Reorganize the filing cabinet at work. Clean out your dresser drawers at home and decide which old clothes to give away. Your digestive system may seem more sensitive than usual. Keep it happy by fixing a delicious but healthy dinner this evening.

Weekly Summary

It may be time to show your more creative side. Learn a new instrument, or take drama or singing lessons. If you feel inhibited, realize that it is only natural at first. You can surprise yourself when you see that you have latent untapped talent in one of these areas. Don't beat yourself up if you're not perfect right at the beginning.

You may be thinking about getting a new pet at this time. If your landlord does not allow pets, there may be other ways to satisfy this desire. Consider volunteering to do some dog walking at the local animal shelter. You can also get some fish or a bird in lieu of a more active pet.

A love relationship may move to the next level this week. Your partner may want a more serious commitment. If you need more time, speak up now. Sit down and have an honest, heart-to-heart talk with your beloved about what you both want from this relationship.

21st Week/May 21–27

Tuesday the 21st. Harmony is likely to reign in your environment. People seem to get along well now. Join friends for lunch and catch up on the latest gossip. Keep your ear to the ground at the office. There may be something big brewing that could make a difference to your career. Cooperate with a spouse this evening.

Wednesday the 22nd. You may be cutting it close with a deadline at work. You should come through in the final stretch, however. Trust the people with whom you are working. A partner may seem more standoffish than usual right now. You should each have your space. Realize that it probably is nothing that you have done. Be sensitive to a friend's concerns.

Thursday the 23rd. Avoid going out of your way to shock people. It may be okay at home, but the boss will not be too happy about it. Join in on a community discussion about how to better your local environment. Your ideas have more merit than you give them credit for. Consider upgrading your current job skills.

Friday the 24th. An old friend may not be as loyal as you would like. It may be time to reassess the friendship. There probably is someone else waiting in the wings who would love to be your friend. You can appreciate beauty in all of its forms now. Visit the art gallery or local museum this afternoon.

Saturday the 25th. A twist of fate can cause a change in plans. Go with the flow on this one. Things can turn out much better than they have previously. You may be the subject of some gossip around the neighborhood now. Just ignore it. If you feed into it, you may end up only propagating untruths. Go out dancing this evening.

Sunday the 26th. A love relationship may be going through some growing pains. Don't let yourself be manipulated through guilt. If you stand up for yourself, your beloved will respect your integrity and self-confidence. Solitude can help you to tune in to your deeper needs right now. Go for a walk in the woods, or meditate by a stream.

Monday the 27th. Things are going your way this holiday. An enhanced sense of combativeness may make people more wary of you than usual. Avoid coming across as aggressive, however. Being assertive should ensure that you get what you want. An attractive stranger may send you over the moon. Reserve judgment until you get to know the person better. Buy a lottery ticket just in case.

Weekly Summary

This can be a good time to double-check all your insurance policies. It may be time to renew or to increase your coverage to better accommodate your current needs. Check out warranties on your appliances, as well as on your computer system. You may want to take something in for some small repair before the warranty expires.

Education is more exciting than usual. You may be considering going back to school full-time to upgrade a current skill. You should do well at this time, as your mind is focused and disciplined. Teachers may find that they have a resurgence of passion for their subject matter, and can inspire others more easily.

Hard work and discipline can work wonders for you in the career area this week. Perhaps these extra efforts went unnoticed in the past. Don't worry; the boss values your contribution very highly. You may get a raise or a promotion as a result. Consistency is what can work for you now.

22nd Week/May 28–June 3

Tuesday the 28th. You can be seen as a pioneer. Don't be afraid to broadcast your ideas, even if they seem rather unconventional. This is a good day for new beginnings. Plant a garden, start a new job, or make amends to your sweetheart. You should be supported in all of these areas. Get some physical exercise this evening.

Wednesday the 29th. Don't take it personally if an acquaintance doesn't appreciate your generosity. Simply acknowledge that you are not going to become close friends. Wear bright colors now. Although you sit in the background more often than not, it may be time to show off a little. You can be seen as an expert in your field.

Thursday the 30th. You seem to be more concerned than usual about your appearance now. Shopping expeditions for new clothes can prove fruitful. Take along a friend for an objective opinion. Personal finances may bear some looking into. Perhaps a revamping of the budget is in order. You may be invited to a celebration of some kind for a friend. Take along some champagne.

Friday the 31st. You feel more dreamy and introspective than usual. Buckling down to work can be difficult. Try to arrange to take the day off. You will be supported in creative or romantic matters. Inspiration can be found from great works of art. Visit the local art gallery for ideas. Wining and dining can fill the bill tonight.

Saturday June 1st. You excel in all manners of communication now. Languages are easy for you. Some of you may be thinking of learning sign language as a new career. You will be kept busy for most of the day running errands and catching up with friends. Say yes to a last minute get-together this evening.

Sunday the 2nd. A love interest may be getting too close for comfort right now. It may be time to have an honest talk. Your powers of observation tend to be fine-tuned at this time. Plant yourself at a table at the local coffee shop and just people-watch. This can make for a very pleasant and interesting afternoon.

Monday the 3rd. The good things in life appeal to you more than usual. Avoid overindulgence, however. It may be better to skip shopping altogether, as you may be prone to impulse buying. A loved one is showering you with words of appreciation and love right now. They will come either in a love letter or in person.

Weekly Summary

Say yes when you are invited to participate in a local think tank. You may feel that you aren't qualified to join such a distinguished group, but give yourself more credit. You know a lot more than you think. Your personal experience is just as valuable as anybody else's is. Realize that you may be seen as someone with a worthwhile opinion.

This can be a time when good things come to you. Others may call it luck, but you may call it your due. A renewal in life can be the result. Share your good fortune with loved ones. You may be the recipient of a large sum of money. Be sure to splurge on yourself a little.

Your energy and enthusiasm will be quite high this week. You do best when you can apply your energy in short spurts. Consistency may not be your strong suit right now. Start projects, but let others finish them. You should do well in sports requiring quick bursts of energy, such as baseball, sprinting, or bike riding.

23rd Week/June 4–10

Tuesday the 4th. You may be thinking about investing in some new furniture for your home. Don't be afraid to get something of quality, even if it is more expensive. This can be a good time to start collecting things that increase in value over time, such as stamps, coins, or items for your hope chest. A relative will abide by your decision tonight.

Wednesday the 5th. Whatever you do, you are certain to do it fast. Avoid pushing others to work as quickly as you do, however; it can only result in resentment. Try to work as autonomously as possible. Don't let a love interest rush you into anything. Although that person may have strong feelings for you, you may need more time to be sure.

Thursday the 6th. This can be a good day to get your hands dirty in the garden. Plant some flowers or vegetables. Your sense of touch may be enhanced now. Get a massage, or give one. Either way you can benefit from the experience. Impress a date with a home-cooked meal this evening. Don't forget the candlelight and wine.

Friday the 7th. The work day may produce some power struggles. Do your best to stay out of them. Get your work done early, and then take the afternoon off if possible. Treat yourself to some lavish entertainment this evening. Attend the opera or a theater performance. A stand-up comedy show can be another option. Just let yourself have some fun.

Saturday the 8th. You may feel a sense of responsibility pulling you to do something that you do not really want to do. It may be necessary to sacrifice your own personal desires for the sake of someone else. On the whole, it will work out to your advantage. Friends tend to be social and chatty. Accept an invitation tonight.

Sunday the 9th. Communications are all too likely to go awry. Be sure to double-check all travel plans and appointments now. Allow extra time to arrive somewhere, as there probably will be traffic snarls. Don't be surprised if your flight is delayed. Just be sure to phone ahead to eliminate any unnecessary waiting. Keep plans as flexible as possible.

Monday the 10th. Whatever you start now is likely to come to a successful conclusion within the month. This can to be a very good time to begin a new course of study, to start writing a book, or to go public with any new business ventures. Siblings are more likely than usual to be part of the scenario.

Weekly Summary

Do your best not to procrastinate at work this week. It may be easier than usual to avoid doing something you would rather not do. Realize that the longer you put it off, the more pressure you will be under when you do it. Consider setting little goals. Accomplishing a little bit each day may make it easier for you to deal with.

A spouse may be acting very possessive. Understand that it may be a matter of feeling insecure. A little reassurance of your feelings can go a long way toward restoring the self-confidence of your love. For now, it will be prudent to avoid talking about how much fun you had when out socializing with friends.

Older parents or relatives can be on your mind. Perhaps they are being more demanding of your time and attention now. You know that you deserve to have a life of your own. Don't let them make you feel guilty. It will not hurt to be more reassuring of your love and devotion of them, however.

24th Week/June 11–17

Tuesday the 11th. You may receive an unexpected gift from a close friend. Accept it graciously, even if there is no special occasion to warrant it. A family member may try to enlist your support in a home renovation project. Give your support, but avoid taking over. A mate may be quite emotionally sensitive now, so offer some extra reassurance.

Wednesday the 12th. You may be able to see a clear vision of your goals for the future. This can help you to make more relevant decisions in the present. You probably will receive an invitation to a swank social event. Brush up on your social skills if necessary. You may be rubbing elbows with someone who can positively affect your future.

Thursday the 13th. Love can be grand at present. Let yourself get caught up in the whirlwind of romance. Big money can be made through a friend at this time. An investment may seem to be too good to be true, but be sure to take advantage of it; as it probably is on the up-and-up. Be sure to set a time frame for repayment if lending money.

Friday the 14th. You are more likely than usual to be psychically perceptive. You can use this gift when dealing with clients, who may be amazed at your sensitivity to their needs. Personal magnetism will be at an all-time high. Wear dark colors to enhance your charisma. You should look good in black, dark green, or burgundy.

Saturday the 15th. You may be making some travel plans. If traveling for business, try to squeeze in an extra couple of days for fun. Be sure to check it out with the boss first, however. Intellectual stimulation may be high on your list of priorities. Visit the local bookstore and treat yourself to a bestseller, or join a current book discussion.

Sunday the 16th. Your ability to be persuasive will be enhanced. Turn on the charm, and friends will be happy to do things your way. You may display some talent with the written word at this time. If you have ever thought about writing, this can be a very auspicious time to give it a try. A night school course can get you started.

Monday the 17th. You can give a good example of grace under pressure now. Last-minute glitches in a project at work may cause others to panic. Your calm control is probably what saves the day. Be objective but supportive when a friend asks your opinion of her new love interest. This person may be around for a while.

Weekly Summary

Self-restraint can be your hidden strength right now. Call upon it when things get chaotic at work. Part of you may want to get involved in office politics, but this would require you to make a stand. Be aware that this may not be the best time to put yourself out on a limb. Timing may be everything right now.

Your kids will follow any example that you set for them this week. Consider getting involved in charity or volunteer work with them. Take the whole family to the local animal shelter and do some dog-walking. The kids will love it. Realize that your attitude about the whole thing can affect them as well.

Avoid committing yourself to any social plans too far ahead of time. You may be about to receive a barrage of social invitations. Try to put off any decisions until the time of an event is closer at hand. Although this may not be your normal way of doing things, it should ensure that you don't miss out on anything important.

25th Week/June 18–24

Tuesday the 18th. You may find yourself thrust into the spotlight in some way. Be humble to avoid resentment from others. You can make money if you are conservative in your investments right now. An older female may have some inside information that can help you to make the right financial decision. Spruce up your living area with some fresh flowers.

Wednesday the 19th. It can be much harder than usual to keep your temper in check. Communication with others can cause you considerable frustration. An urge to do everything at once will only deplete your energy. A calm, consistent approach should get you to where you want to go. Channel some of your aggression into athletics or some other type of physical endeavor.

Thursday the 20th. An optimistic attitude can win you allies. Confidence in yourself can better allow you to try new things and to take chances. You may discover new things about yourself in the process. Watch for a tendency toward overoptimism, however. Make an extra effort to assess all the angles before plunging in.

Friday the 21st. You seem to have a more deliberate attitude than usual. Deep and serious discussions will be stimulating now. A need to figure out another person's motivations can have you playing detective. You have the ability to get to the crux of matters now. Money prospects can be abundant if you know where to look. Trust your intuition.

Saturday the 22nd. A love relationship is likely to go to a deeper level. A partner may take a special interest in your thoughts and feelings. Be sure to share. A bond of greater trust and intimacy can be formed as a result. Use your creativity and imagination to solve a problem involving children. Even you may be amazed at how well the kids respond to you.

Sunday the 23rd. Someone important from your past may make an unexpected appearance. Seeing the person again may force you to confront some unresolved issues. Once dealt with, you will feel a greater sense of peace. You may be feeling pressured to act quickly in regard to an important decision. Remember that it is your decision, so take you time with it.

Monday the 24th. Intense emotions from a loved one could catch you off-guard. You probably had no idea that the person's feelings were so strong. Give assurance of your support, and he or she may feel more free to divulge feelings to you in the future as a result. All creative mental work is favored now. Open up to new information and enlarge your views.

Weekly Summary

Handle bill payments, visit a notary, take care of official paperwork. As this week starts, you can get organized on legal paperwork that has been sitting around for a while. Legal advisors will be quite helpful. You will get better answers this week that can help you with important decisions, such as setting up wills. People in charge may take you under their wings.

You may be feeling uncharacteristically obsessed with an idea or goal this week. It will be best to keep your thoughts and feelings under wraps. Don't let others spoil your enthusiasm for attempting something out of the ordinary, such as winning the championship in a public contest. What seems important to you may be dismissed as impossible by family or friends.

Don't feel inhibited if you are attracted to a much younger individual at this time. Age should not make a difference to the heart. Perhaps you are needing someone who can brighten and lighten you. Don't let the old taboos prevent you from enjoying a new relationship that may turn out to be quite special.

26th Week/June 25–July 1

Tuesday the 25th. Helping others can be what opens doors for you. Your intention may be just to help out others less fortunate. It may be this very selfless attitude that gets you noticed. You are seen as someone with integrity and compassion now. An offer of a new job may come your way. Although it is unusual, consider its possibilities.

Wednesday the 26th. Communications are more likely than usual to go awry. Be especially careful to be clear and succinct when imparting information to someone important. This can ensure that your meaning comes across without confusion. Take your time when making expensive purchases. Be sure that this decision is consistent with your long-term financial goals. Stay home this evening.

Thursday the 27th. You may receive recognition for efforts made in the workplace. Accept your kudos graciously. Your charisma is very appealing to others at this time. Someone close may be trying to win your approval. Let people know that they don't have to try so hard. Learning should be easier than usual now. Take a class or study on your own.

Friday the 28th. A male figure may be acting as if he has some kind of authority over you. He is likely to be trying to intimidate you. Don't be afraid to speak up. He should soon see that his patronizing attitude may be getting him nowhere. You may receive inside information regarding a project close to your heart. Use it discreetly.

Saturday the 29th. You probably will hear words of love from someone special. Repay the sentiment. Expect to be kept busy with errands and appointments this afternoon. Take the time to stop and chat along the way, however. Join a friend at a lecture or seminar this evening. It could open up a whole new area of interest for you.

Sunday the 30th. You may feel the need to take a mini-vacation. This can be the perfect time for a road trip. Offer to take guests sightseeing. This can help you to be a tourist in your own town and get to see the places close to home that you usually take for granted. Physical activity is favored. Join a friend for a tennis game, or go for a swim at the pool.

Monday July 1st. Get ready for a busy day. Things probably are crazy in the office. Deadlines are looming ever nearer. If you're running behind schedule, you had better catch up before it gets out of hand. Folks can be impulsive now, so be prepared for a change of plans. You're likely to have some extra nervous energy, so go out for a nice walk or some exercise if you have time.

Weekly Summary

A disagreement with a sibling can wind up being a positive experience in the end. By voicing your opinions, you release tension and let others know how you feel. You should have lots of energy to work around the house now. Complete any projects that may be half-finished. Don't be bothered by a youngster's outburst. If you keep calm, you can probably defuse any difficulties.

Delays and mix-ups can cause frustration this week. Misunderstandings can occur, and things can be misplaced or lost. Careful planning can halt potential problems. Don't believe everything you hear. Someone probably is exaggerating. Try to participate in a neighborhood event. If you do, don't get involved in gossip or speaking negatively about others.

You can expect your finances to improve this week, however minor it may seem. Your willingness to go the extra mile makes all the difference. You can finally come to agreement on a deal you have been wanting for a long time. Have an important person over for dinner to make a good impression. You can be lucky in love if you take a chance; you will never know if you don't try.

27th Week/July 2–8

Tuesday the 2nd. People will find you engaging, charming, and will enjoy talking to you. This can work very well if you are trying to get a favor from someone. Family should respond positively to your ideas. Arguments can be settled easily. This is a better time than usual to mix business and pleasure. With a sweet smile, you can attract a new romantic interest.

Wednesday the 3rd. Your restlessness is best put to use around the house or doing something productive. You will feel really good once you see what you have accomplished. Hobbies can be especially fulfilling. It is possible that you will lose your temper with a young person. Keep this in mind. If you start to feel irritated, count to ten. Try to relax with a good book this evening.

Thursday the 4th. On this Independence Day family members will appreciate any one-on-one time they can get with you. Schedule time like this if you can. You married Capricorns may want to consider what your partner has been going through lately. Perhaps your nurturing is just what's needed. Don't forget to take some time out to pamper yourself, too. Buy yourself something that smells wonderful.

Friday the 5th. Home and family will be at the top of your list. Small gestures can go a long way toward making someone special feel loved and appreciated. Relationships are in focus as well. Those of you who are married can impress your spouse with romance or a kind word. You single Capricorns may want to get out of the house tonight.

Saturday the 6th. Dreaming about someone special can make your day more pleasant. You may feel the pang of love lost or unrequited. Your imagination can be in peak form. This can be a great time for you artists, musicians, and writers. A child in your life may be trying to tell you something and you're not getting it. Team sports are a good way to blow off steam.

Sunday the 7th. This active day will not necessarily be a fulfilling one. A long holiday weekend for some of you will be neither restful nor peaceful. You are restless. Keep your schedule flexible if you are between visits. Family may try to pin you down to a definite time and place. A partner or a friend can be equally insistent on a special date with you. A young one's humor will put small discontent into a happy perspective.

Monday the 8th. This can be quite a productive day for you. Your restlessness virtually guarantees that you will get lots done. Make sure you have a focus, though. All this energy may be wasted if you don't. Channeled correctly, however, you can do some really excellent work. Research is featured. Others will respond to your upbeat approach. You can be pleasantly surprised.

Weekly Summary

Those of you who are parents may notice a difference in the way you and your spouse want kids to be managed. An argument or disagreement is possible. You can find it tough to enforce rules. Remember that your children look to you for guidance. Routines can be disrupted now; but if you get right back into the rhythm, it shouldn't make too much difference.

If you have been disorganized lately, you will be feeling the effects now. Paperwork and important objects can be lost if you're not careful. You can be late for appointments if you're not on the ball. Get your act together and you will feel much better. This is not the week to waste time or miss opportunities. Self-discipline can be improved now.

This week can be a fantastic time for getting rid of unwanted items. Advertising is favored. Ask for top dollar, and dicker from there. You may buy some good tools or other equipment to replace ones you are no longer using. Pay close attention to new people who come into your life now. This is also a time when you can meet someone who will become very important in your life.

28th Week/July 9–15

Tuesday the 9th. Be realistic about what you can and cannot accomplish. Avoid both giving and receiving unsolicited advice. People sometimes are better off working things out on their own. Organizing and self-improvement are featured. A job well done brings a sense of satisfaction. Have dinner with a co-worker or employee if you can. You may come up with a fantastic new idea.

Wednesday the 10th. Work hard to complete unfinished business. Make absolutely sure to proofread and edit any outgoing documents. Your work can come under scrutiny. By this evening you may need some deep relaxation. Plan a date tonight if possible. Go somewhere inspiring. An uplifting play, concert, or movie should be fun and as well as relaxing.

Thursday the 11th. A platonic friendship may lead to more if you're not careful. However, if that's exactly what you have in mind, this will be your day. Think carefully before you leap into the unknown, however. There may be forces outside your control that come into play. Socializing with co-workers or other acquaintances can be more fun than you may have thought.

Friday the 12th. If you're married, it is important that you spend time with your spouse. It can be all too easy to get caught up in work, school, or social lives and forget about your partner. Plan a date where you and your loved one can do something that is mutually enjoyable. You single Capricorns may want to plan a day doing something you love, be it gardening, reading, or whatever.

Saturday the 13th. You may be asked to make a loan or otherwise handle another's money or possessions. Make sure you have a firm agreement. A written contract would be the best if possible. Be sure to include a payment plan and any unusual details. You need to be protected right now. Spending time with friends brings rewards. Try something you have never done before.

Sunday the 14th. A visit to a park or ethnic neighborhood can be a great way to spend a sunny afternoon. Or perhaps you can get a bunch of old friends together to toss around a ball. You don't have to spend a lot of money to have a good time. A picnic can be easily arranged. Get everyone to pitch in so that you don't have to do all the work yourself.

Monday the 15th. Your personal reality may be different from that of a parent or authority figure. Try to be flexible and allow for differences. You may find yourself giving some thought to what the future holds for you in the area of career or self-improvement. Allow your mind to wander and daydream. You just may come up with a creative idea that works well.

Weekly Summary

An inheritance can be in the cards at this time in your life. Disagreements with family members or other heirs may be on the verge of resolving. Certainly you can help this along more than you realize. It can be very helpful to get the opinion of a trusted and disinterested third party. Mediation may be an option, and it can be an excellent idea. Try to get a referral if this is the case.

You probably will be busier than usual this week. Business can take you out of town. You may not be too happy about it if you're living out of a suitcase. Try to make the best of it, however. You can be meeting new people who give you a new perspective on some of the deeper meanings in life. Open your mind to new ideas and philosophies. You don't have to believe everything you hear, but at least listen.

Give your attention to the goals you would like to achieve in the month ahead. Do you know what you really want? Plant the seeds now. Make a game plan and then follow through. What is your first move? This is a creative time, so make the best of it. Your visualizations can become manifestations. Start taking steps toward making it so.

29th Week/July 16–22

Tuesday the 16th. Start projects that help meet your ambitions. A shift toward money and career goals may become apparent. Long-term financial goals will benefit from your attention. Insurance, taxes, and legal matters may be in focus. You may be asked to help someone else in these areas. Help employees and co-workers get ahead. Together you can support each other.

Wednesday the 17th. Write down a set of goals and stick to it, even if it's only a to-do list. You can get a lot accomplished if you are focused. You may even want to review your general goals and ambitions and make a list of these. With patience and persistence, you are sure to make it happen. A youngster may be watching you carefully. Try to set a good example.

Thursday the 18th. It's time to get serious. Be practical about what you hope to achieve. Your hard work and persistence will surely pay off. Don't be misled by get-rich-quick schemes. Act cautiously and deliberately at this time, not impulsively. There is a tendency for you to be quite hasty, so try not to take on too much work. Avoid making promises you can't keep.

Friday the 19th. You will get more work done if you enlist the help of others. Projects involving teamwork can move right along. You should be able to get the cooperation of others on the job or at school. If you are single, you may meet someone through a neighborhood or community function. Loosen up and try to have a little fun if you're out and around.

Saturday the 20th. Try to take some time out for fun. The theater, concerts, any kind of exciting event can be in the cards. You're likely to enjoy mixed company. Take another's pride into account. Egos are easily wounded. A fascinating conversation can lead to more than you bargained for. You may volunteer for a job you thought you would never do.

Sunday the 21st. Try to get away from it all. Allow yourself to daydream. Out of dreams come ideas. Be creative. How would you like situations in your life to be? What would be the best possible outcome of a situation in your life? Reflection and meditation can bring answers. Your dreams are powerful. Listen carefully to your inner voice. Believe in yourself.

Monday the 22nd. Your kindness and sense of humor can be really noticed. An opportunity to patch up a miscommunication may be presented. Don't let your pride stand in the way. Sometimes it is better to have peace than to be right. It's to your advantage to keep the lines of communication open from now on. Relax this evening at home with loved ones if you can.

Weekly Summary

A pet project may be more work than you thought. It will all depend on how much effort and thought you are putting into it. Investments and savings plans can be made successfully now. It is possible for new and exciting things to happen. However, get-rich-quick schemes will best be avoided. Take it slow and play it safe. Your actions will pay off in the end.

Try to complete an old project before moving on to a new one. It may be time to clean out the closets. Going through boxes and getting rid of things you no longer need can have a very positive effect on you. You may even want to sell something to pick up a few extra bucks. You should have the extra energy needed to get things done. However, don't forget to have a little fun.

You may find yourself gravitating toward a certain spiritual group or a church or synagogue function.

You're likely to be feeling the pull toward understanding the more illusive parts of life. Some of you Capricorns can fill this void by spending time in nature, or by doing charity work. Devoting time or money to those less fortunate has a way of warming the heart.

30th Week/July 23–29

Tuesday the 23rd. Problems involving business can be easily solved. A simple change in your routine will make all the difference. Get organized. Put in the extra effort required. It will be worth it when you start seeing results. You will be able to count on a female relative to be supportive. Your involvement with public relations or publicity is favored.

Wednesday the 24th. You may have unnecessary anxiety early in the day, probably caused by financial pressures. These worries pass quickly, leaving you with a greater understanding of your situation. If you're away from home, don't forget to relax and have fun. If you find yourself alone tonight, escape with a good book or film. If you're out, try a foreign movie or sports event.

Thursday the 25th. This can be a good day to get a haircut or a makeover. Try a few different styles when shopping for clothes. You will want to make yourself look extra good before going to a dinner tonight. There can be someone interesting giving you signals. Flirting with that special person can could make for an evening to remember. A joke can break the ice.

Friday the 26th. Larger-than-life appetites can get you into trouble. Be careful when it comes to eating, drinking, and spending money. You may find yourself trying to impress your friends with your good taste. You Capricorns sometimes try too hard to impress others, often to your own detriment. When it comes to your waistline and wallet, a little goes a long way.

Saturday the 27th. It may be easy for others to misconstrue your words. Crossed or missed communications are possible. Speak clearly and concisely, especially where financial matters are concerned. Put important matters into writing and make sure they're delivered properly. Your message can be received wrong or not at all. Confirm the arrival of important correspondence.

Sunday the 28th. You may feel the need to ask for a favor. People can be a little evasive, so if you do, try to make clear exactly what you need. Siblings and cousins may be more than willing to help you out. Be sure you make it worth their while. A neighbor may not see eye-to-eye with you when it comes to community improvements, yard maintenance, or the like.

Monday the 29th. You may want to spend some time fixing things up at home, such as decorating or the purchase of art. The change will do you good. A perfect day might include some kind of home improvement. Afterward, invite a friend or two over for supper or drinks. Enjoy your new luxurious surroundings. Take responsibility for your own actions, not for those of someone else.

Weekly Summary

Your confidence, optimistic attitude, and talents can get you far. If you are aware of your unique personal talent, make a point to use it. If not, you may be able to discover it now. You may also be interested in romance. A close friend can have some good advice for you in this department. Social interests may keep you very busy this week. Avoid overdoing it.

You may decide now to mix business and pleasure. Just get all your important work out of the way first. Routine chores can seem burdensome and may need extra attention. However, when finished, they can give you a great sense of satisfaction. An office romance, though tempting, can land you into more trouble than it's worth. A new health regimen is favored.

Hard work and motivation will start to pay off now. Use excess energy this week to clear up any organizational matters. It pays to get your act together. Clear your office of any unfinished paperwork. Phone calls returned will bring rewards. Avoid being overcritical with co-workers and employees at this time. If you haven't already done so, vacation planning can be on the agenda.

31st Week/July 30–August 5

Tuesday the 30th. Your mind will be especially sharp at present. Make note of creative ideas. Put them to use. Write them down for later if you cannot work them out now. Call, write, fax, or e-mail people. Talking with people helps you to work out the details. A sibling or cousin can be supportive and helpful. You may enjoy a comedy act or a funny movie tonight.

Wednesday the 31st. Your abundant physical energy is useful on the job or in doing chores. This may be annoying to those close to you who are lazy. Your upbeat mood wins the confidence of an older gentleman or someone important. An optimistic attitude saves the day. You may be making travel plans. You will not want to stay at home if you have other options.

Thursday August 1st. Your sense of fairness will help out when you are asked to settle a disagreement between co-workers. Be sure you hear both sides of the story before you make any assumptions. Pay attention to any nagging feelings regarding your health or mental state. A visit to an alternative health practitioner can set your mind at ease. Get some exercise.

Friday the 2nd. Do try to take some time away from working or household duties to enjoy the finer things in life. Luxuries of all types will be appealing. Indulge in good company, fine food, and wonderful music or art. Friends and lovers alike can be a pleasure to be around, so bask in the warmth of their affection. If you're home alone, phone someone if you can.

Saturday the 3rd. These can be wonderfully romantic and friendly times. You are lucky indeed if you have someone with whom to share them. If you do, make plans to be with your special someone, and do something special. Those of you who are single, make sure you are with friends or family. Perhaps you can meet someone special. Even if you don't, you will enjoy the company of others.

Sunday the 4th. Complete a project you have already started before you move on to the next one. Plenty of energy will be needed to complete a difficult job. Older people and those in authority can be very helpful. A young man is likely to surprise you by being more mature than you expect. Passions can run quite high, so channel them in a positive manner.

Monday the 5th. What a perfect day for love and romance. If you don't have a sweetie, or cannot be with yours, romance yourself. Try to pamper yourself with whatever it is that makes you feel good. Even if you are busy and don't have much time, you can think of something to do that makes you feel wonderful. Do something to make your living environment nicer.

Weekly Summary

It is time to get organized. Clean out your closets, so to speak. You feel good when you are being productive. Spend time in the garden if you have one. Any do-it-yourself or craft project can be rewarding. Avoid being overly critical of yourself or others. You should be able to borrow or lend money now with good results. Just make sure to get it in writing.

Relations with your significant other will take top billing now. Take a few minutes to think of something wonderful you can do together. Include a gift or gesture that makes your loved one feel like the most wonderful person alive, at least in your eyes. You're sure to feel rewarded when you see your partner's response. Single Capricorns can play the field.

A difficult situation may arise this week with an older person. A conflict with a parent or elder can be very intense. Your instinct is to hide away, which would only make matters worse. Keep the lines of communication open. It could merely be that you need to get something out in the open. Don't be afraid to talk about things. Take responsibility for your actions.

32nd Week/August 6–12

Tuesday the 6th. If it seems that your spouse is overreacting, you could be right. People can get downright touchy now. You may feel like putting on some kid gloves and then walking on eggshells. Any difficulty will be short-lived, however. Tonight can be quite passionate if you want it to be. You may enjoy viewing a mystery movie, opera, or sports event.

Wednesday the 7th. Pay extra attention to a fascinating new person that you meet. He or she can be key to a career or social improvement. It would be easy to miss this opportunity if you aren't aware of it. If you do meet such a person, start a conversation just to see where it leads. You may be surprised. Don't get discouraged if you get sidetracked.

Thursday the 8th. Someone may be relying on you to solve some financial problems. Feel free to lend a hand. Even better, educate the person to take care of personal matters. It's possible to be both nurturing and authoritative. This can work best for both of you. A long-distance trip can be both fun and informative. Don't be surprised if plans change suddenly.

Friday the 9th. You may be involved in making travel arrangements or planning an excursion of some kind. Make sure you remember all the details if you can. You're likely to find yourself awfully busy, and it may be difficult to focus. Even those of you with no plans can quickly find yourself involved in something or other, probably of a social nature.

Saturday the 10th. A getaway to a beach or relaxing resort can be absolutely perfect this weekend. A walk in a natural setting is uplifting. Bring along a camera, some music, or a journal if you are so inclined. Religious, spiritual, and creative pursuits are in focus now. Your dreams and meditations can be revealing. If you must stay home, try to relax and enjoy yourself.

Sunday the 11th. Anything you start now should last a long time. This can work for or against you. As the saying goes, be careful what you wish for because you may get it. The key words here are caution and conservative. This is an excellent day to lose yourself in romance. You can earn points with someone special by making a nice home-cooked meal tonight.

Monday the 12th. Expect to be quite active now. A chance encounter with an acquaintance is probable. This can be beneficial. A government authority or organization can be quite helpful to a group effort that you are involved in. A new agreement of some kind with in-laws may be made. Defuse complaints by listening and responding quickly.

Weekly Summary

Joint financial concerns are likely to come up at this time. The answer may be simpler than you think. Talk it over with the other person involved and you may come up with a solution. Cooperative ventures are favored now, so get together with another to start up a profitable new project. You may want to think twice about taking on a new project if it involves borrowing money.

Your career seems to be improving, but how is your family life going? It can be tempting to ignore that part. It may seem like things will just take care of themselves. Take a few minutes out to think about relatives or your roommates. Have you been fair and considerate in all of your dealings with them? If not, it's never too late to try to make up for it.

That isn't to say that you should ignore your ambitions. On the contrary, this can be an excellent time to make progress as far as your goals and dreams are concerned. You can grow in leaps and bounds if you are willing to do a little work. Luck is a mixture of preparedness and opportunity. The call of a foreign land may be strong. Perhaps a vacation is in order.

33rd Week/August 13–19

Tuesday the 13th. Hanging out with friends can be appealing. You will enjoy conversing with others, whether about trivial or deeper matters. Phone someone you like and plan lunch if you can. You are feeling quite ambitious now. Think about what you really need to accomplish at this time. Give some thought to getting yourself or your ideas out into the world.

Wednesday the 14th. You might leap gung-ho into a situation involving a club or other group without realizing just what you're in for. You're may be a bit overenthusiastic without even having all of the facts. Try not to make any promises or overextend yourself, or you may be sorry. You may not get much business done in meetings. Try to focus on the matter at hand.

Thursday the 15th. Take a few minutes out for reflecting on your current life circumstances. Are things going the way you like in the different areas of your life? This can be the right day for reviewing and making changes. Getting together with friends for a group activity can be fulfilling. Pay attention to nonverbal clues like body language to get the real truth.

Friday the 16th. Try to get a rest if at all possible. Those of you who absolutely must work will feel better if you can do some relaxation exercises or try to lie down for a few minutes. Your dreams may be quite strong over the next day or so. Consciously remembering and analyzing them can be insightful. A visit to an elderly relative or neighbor may be on the agenda.

Saturday the 17th. Try to take some time out for fun. The theater, concerts, any kind of exciting event can bring much pleasure. You will enjoy mixed company.

Don't be too proud. Your ego can easily be wounded. Ignore gossip and rumors that are going around if you don't want to get involved. A fascinating conversation may lead to romance.

Sunday the 18th. This promises to be a nice pleasant day. You will feel lucky in just about every area of your life. You single Capricorns should pay close attention if someone seems to be looking your way. Being shy will not do when opportunity presents itself. Decorating projects can bring excellent results. Family time is especially featured. Go easy on the sweets.

Monday the 19th. It's possible to feel more emotional than usual. Little things like sad stories can get to you. This may cause you to contribute to a charity or volunteer your time, which would be rewarding. You can absorb the moods of people you're with, so make sure they are upbeat types. Negative folks can really get you down; avoid them if at all possible.

Weekly Summary

An opportunity to make more money honestly should not be ignored. You may find yourself starting something new this week. If you currently have one source of income, you can find something else to add to that. You may be offered something that seems too good to be true. If it does, it probably is. Use discrimination, and you will be less likely to be disappointed.

Try to take some time out for meditation or reflection this week. The busier you are, the more you will need to relax. This will help you to feel more confident, and you can draw people to you. You can promote yourself, your ideas, or product now if you have prepared properly. Even if you don't feel completely confident, you can still get out and meet people.

A child or young man is featured in your life. A great creative idea may come from it. Take some time out this week to have some fun. Board games, computer games, and other forms of mental stimulation are featured. What one thing is really relaxing and fun for you? Try to do that very thing now. Reading a nonfiction book can be enlightening.

34th Week/August 20–26

Tuesday the 20th. Sometimes you seem to meet people everywhere you go. This can very well be one of those days. An unusual or eccentric stranger may turn out to be a fantastic contact. This person can introduce you to other people who will prove indispensable. You may be held responsible for keeping the peace at home tonight. Look at all sides before you pass judgment.

Wednesday the 21st. Try to avoid stretching the truth in order to make your stories more interesting. By the same token, don't swallow others' tales hook, line, and sinker. If you find yourself in a fairy-tale or whirlwind romance, enjoy it. Don't get caught up in fantasy or expectations, however. Take things slow and easy. In the meantime, some candlelight and roses never hurt anyone.

Thursday the 22nd. You may be able to make a really smart financial move. If you haven't given much thought to retirement income, this is a good time to do so. This day is also excellent for starting projects that have to do with the public. You may be involved with media or publicity in some fashion. Allow yourself to enjoy some simple luxuries at some point.

Friday the 23rd. Make necessary adjustments to a project that was started approximately three weeks ago.

You may feel as though you have come up against a brick wall. Don't let it discourage you too much. Find a way to climb up and over that wall. Don't worry; it is really possible to overcome this obstacle. Where there's a will, there's a way. If you believe in yourself, your goal will soon be in sight.

Saturday the 24th. You are likely to move too fast and in too many different directions. While conversations may be interesting, don't let the boss catch you talking on company time. You could be embarrassed later if you hear your stories repeated. If you aren't paying attention, you may also slip up and divulge information that would be best kept under wraps.

Sunday the 25th. Be careful with hasty words. A family member or close friend is awfully sensitive and can easily be hurt. You may unintentionally say the wrong thing. If this happens, a quick response from you will set things right. Dinner out with a group of friends or business associates is a definite possibility. Try to listen more than you talk. Pay attention to body language.

Monday the 26th. It may take an extra cup of coffee to get you started this morning. It probably will be a quiet atmosphere in the office. Work can be slow, so have alternative activities to do. If you have a good book to escape into, you can spend hours off in another world. Screen your telephone calls if you don't want interruptions. Watch your food and alcohol consumption tonight.

Weekly Summary

Community or neighborhood projects may be on the agenda. Volunteer some time if you can to help make things successful. If you have no extra time, perhaps you can donate some cash or come up with another creative way to help. All charitable activities are favored. Those of you who have sales ability may be able to raise money for a good cause.

This can be an auspicious time to start thinking about a new business or career project. You Capricorns make good entrepreneurs and managers, and you can prove that now. Working from the home is a possibility. You may wish to consider looking into it further if you haven't already. You're likely to feel more in control of your destiny now, so go for it.

You can come up with a different idea for making money or improving your financial situation as well. Try to avoid talking about it much with others, however. Your idea may not yet be viable or you may not be ready to take the necessary steps to make it happen. If this is the case, sharing your idea could cause it to be used by someone else. You would be better off to study and prepare for a later date.

35th Week/August 27–September 2

Tuesday the 27th. Energetic and ambitious, there will not be much you cannot do if you apply yourself. You should be able to visualize and manifest. You may want to enlist the opinion of a trusted friend if you're not sure of your next move. You may meet someone who will play an important role in your life over the next two weeks. Your partner may need more attention.

Wednesday the 28th. Your may find yourself preoccupied with career or work issues. Remember your domestic responsibilities, however. Both are important, but your family may need to take priority at this time. If you must work overtime, try to quit as early as possible. Make sure you take some time out. You may be missing more than you realize.

Thursday the 29th. Focus on home. A family member may have a perspective different from yours. It will be up to you to tell your side as you see it. It can be difficult to devote yourself to responsibilities. You can be sidetracked by someone who is more interested in pleasure than in business. Something you have lost may be found if you keep your eyes open.

Friday the 30th. You may find that your energy level is low. If this is the case, try to get some rest. You will probably be in great demand at work. Take care of your duties first, and then play. Another option is to take frequent breaks. A disagreement with a man is possible. Don't let him get the best of you. A social evening is possible, but watch what you eat and drink.

Saturday the 31st. Pay attention to the little voices inside your head. Your intuition is likely to be right on the money when it comes to love. You may find that someone special is looking your way. Be receptive to opportunities for romance. Creative pursuits will be beneficial. Nurture a child's individuality. Dancing and enjoying music can be on the agenda.

Sunday September 1st. Spend the day taking care of details if you can. The next week or probably will be quite busy. This can be your last chance to take care of such things. Nervous tension can make you feel ill. If you have someone to pamper you, take advantage and let yourself relax and be waited on. If not, you can treat yourself. Try to eat healthy food.

Monday the 2nd. An issue involving a co-worker may be on your mind this Labor Day. You can be feeling rather suspicious. This can work for you or against you. Your mind should be very sharp and excellent for detective work and researching. Just remember to be fair.

This can be a day to go shopping and spend money, since you are not prone to overspend at this time.

Weekly Summary

If you take on a major project this week, try to stick to your plans. It can be all too easy to want to add to them. Things have a way of getting out of control if you're not careful. If you think you're going over your budget, review it before it gets out of hand. Alternatively, you may find you're running out of time or going over deadline. You can catch up if you hurry.

If you are a student or working on a research project, the start of this week can make you feel as if you are losing ground rather than gaining. Perhaps you are gathering too much information. Stick to your essential theme, and formulate a step-by-step process. Discard nonessential or extra paperwork and you will be able to turn in stronger work. Don't hesitate to ask for help.

Whether you have a large party or a romantic date for two in your plans, either should go smoothly. In fact, leisure time is important now. If you feel like being alone, that's fine too. Solitary time can recharge your batteries. You may want to take yourself out on a date to do something special. You don't have to spend lots of money. A visit to a park can be just perfect.

36th Week/September 3–9

Tuesday the 3rd. Relationships are particularly intense, but rewarding. Kindness to a loved one has its own rewards. An older person or parent brings news. This message can make all your recent efforts seem worthwhile. Have patience tonight. Be grateful for the support of those around you. Show them how much they are appreciated.

Wednesday the 4th. Partnerships are featured now. If you're entering into a new one, try to make sure you know all the facts. There is a tendency to view situations through rose-colored glasses. You may have romance on your mind. If so, plan a nice evening out or in, complete with music and candlelight. Make an effort to have a special night, and you will be rewarded for it.

Thursday the 5th. A new venture or project seems to be quite promising, so much so that you may wish to get a friend involved. You can benefit through teamwork at this time. As goals are met, you enjoy pride in your achievement. Interesting news can affect your decision on a matter involving your job. You may be traveling soon, so be prepared.

Friday the 6th. You may find it difficult to keep a secret to yourself. If so, ask a friend not to confide in you. By the same token, be careful whom you are talking to and what about. You might not like it if it comes full circle. Don't give in to impulsive purchases. You can end up wondering why you bought an outfit just to have it hang in the closet.

Saturday the 7th. Being somewhat impulsive, you should be in the mood for some real fun. Activities like games, shopping, and flirtatious encounters are great as long as you don't go overboard. You married Capricorns can take joy in pleasing your partner. Some Capricorns can look forward to a promising New Year as they celebrate Rosh Hashanah.

Sunday the 8th. Cooperation can be hampered a little by your inclination to argue over detail. You may feel irritated by those closest to you. If so, take a deep breath and count to ten. It should pass quickly. A close encounter with someone magnetic is possible. Be careful with whom you flirt. Burn off excess physical energy and frustrations through exercise and competitive sports.

Monday the 9th. You may be tempted to take a gamble with a career move. Covert action, such as sending your resume to a competing company, can have a way of backfiring now. Even if things seem really clear, you never know what may come up. It's better to wait a day or two. Children can be most enjoyable tonight. Family activities are a good way to spend your time.

Weekly Summary

Friendships will take top billing toward the end of the week. You may be called, literally or figuratively, to give assistance to someone in need. Don't hesitate to help out a true and loyal friend. By the same token, you may benefit from the help of another. Groups can be great too. Social events should be fun and perhaps even exciting. Don't be too shy.

You seem to be getting more and more busy. It is tempting to take on more than you can reasonably handle. Don't be afraid to say no if you aren't sure you can follow through on a promise. When dealing with those who hold authority over you, remember to show utmost respect. You can be feeling too confident and forget whom you're dealing with.

You may not be at your most romantic self, so give yourself a break. Those of you who are married may be feeling pressured to give more of yourself than you feel you can at this time. Your energies, both physical and emotional, may be low as a result of many outside pressures. However, a loving gesture toward your mate can go far toward keeping the home fires burning.

37th Week/September 10–16

Tuesday the 10th. Don't expect your routine to operate smoothly all day. Unexpected surprises can come your way. You may face power struggles with an over-confident or frustrated person. You can save the day by remaining calm and grounded. If you must lay blame, be sure you can back your words up with facts. For fun, you may enjoy a mystery movie or suspense novel.

Wednesday the 11th. Your dreams may seem far away, but they're closer than you think. With hard work, nothing can stop you. This is just the attitude it takes to succeed. Groups and associations can be very beneficial. A meeting can be productive. Move with caution into a potential new project if it involves others as partners. You may be dealing with someone who is not entirely on the level.

Thursday the 12th. If someone is absent at work, you may be asked to take on additional responsibilities. Be honest if you haven't done the job before. Otherwise you may be left with more responsibility than you can easily cope with. Friends will be generous with compliments. You can be pleasantly surprised if someone picks up the tab at lunch.

Friday the 13th. Your affiliation with a group or association can lead to a new job opportunity. Charity work becomes important. You can make a bigger difference than you think. Your special talent is valuable to others. Take advantage of any chances you get to share it. You're likely to enjoy being the center of attention. Don't be shy when it comes to romance.

Saturday the 14th. This is a restless day filled with loads of physical energy. Get out and around if you can. Your social side needs to be expressed sometimes. A short journey can be quite wonderful. A telephone conversation brings much-needed camaraderie. This will be a good time to go shopping for new clothes or get a haircut. Why not try a whole new style?

Sunday the 15th. Your contribution can really make a difference in a group situation. Originality and a pioneering spirit are exactly what's needed. Don't be afraid to make your ideas known. People will be receptive. This can be a favorable day for socializing. A close friend can use your undivided attention. Be tactful and diplomatic if you must criticize.

Monday the 16th. An impulsive mood can lead to your spending frivolously. You may be tempted to buy lottery tickets or play games of chance. Your odds are a little better than usual. But don't go overboard. Don't pass judgment on some interesting news regarding a family member until you know the whole story. Those observing Yom Kippur will emphasize forgiveness.

Weekly Summary

Your goals and aspirations can take on more meaning this week. While it's good to stretch your boundaries in order to succeed, you may be tempted to do or say something that doesn't quite feel comfortable. Follow your inner voice rather than risk it. Let honesty and integrity be your guide. You will regret it if you go against your better judgment.

Friends can be a great source of inspiration and help at this time. Confiding in someone you trust can ease a burden you may have been carrying for quite a while. By the same token, you may become the confidant of someone you know. Try to suspend judgment if on the receiving end of a confession. Your opinion matters less than your support and understanding.

You may find that you're happier behind the scenes rather than being the center of attention. In romance, stereotypical activities like walking on the beach, gazing at the sunset, and holding hands are all they're cracked up to be. Being around groups socially will be more fulfilling toward the first part of the week, as after that you may be in a more solitary frame of mind.

38th Week/September 17–23

Tuesday the 17th. Exercise care in financial matters. A conservative approach will be better than a risky one. Make sure your accounts are all up to date and bills paid. In romance, keep your feet planted firmly on the ground. Although it is easy to do so now, do not avoid fiscal responsibilities. Running from these obligations only makes them more difficult later.

Wednesday the 18th. Results of your recent efforts should start to come in now. Whether it's what you hoped for remains to be seen. It's probably not too late to change the outcome if you think you need to. A young man may have an important message. Make sure you listen to him. Avoid unnecessary risks, especially when it comes to personal or physical safety.

Thursday the 19th. If intuition is telling you one thing while logic is telling you another, wait for more information before you act. No one will fault you if you take your time coming to a conclusion, hopefully the right one. A secret affair is not so secret anymore, as one of your confidants cannot resist talking. Continued luck is yours if you play your cards close to your vest.

Friday the 20th. Brothers, sisters, and cousins can play a role in your life now. People may have a better sense of humor than you. You're more likely to be impatient. There is a slight danger of being stubborn and argumentative. If you see this happening, change the subject quickly or exit the room gracefully. An older woman may be very helpful to you now.

Saturday the 21st. Minor trouble with a family member or housemate is possible. You may say the wrong thing unintentionally. The situation can try your patience. Sensitive and considerate discussion is called for. Choose your words carefully, as you may have a tendency to put your foot in your mouth. On the plus side, it may be advantageous to finally clear the air.

Sunday the 22nd. Capricorn cool will be an asset today when others are edgy and impatient. The more things are hurried, the less likely they will get done without hassle. Stay calm and collected to avert mishap or loss. Tempers flare in close relationships. Listen to the opposition, for it can motivate you to be at your best. Prepare thoroughly for any legal proceedings coming up. Don't try to second-guess the outcome.

Monday the 23rd. Tensions in the home this morning will be short-lived. Avoid getting involved in other people's arguments, especially at work or in close quarters. Something that was lost recently can be found again. Try looking under furniture or in drawers. A newly developed technology may hold the answer to a problem at work. Investigate before you invest.

Weekly Summary

Change seems to be in the air at this time. Some restlessness, both personally and professionally, is indicated. But a desire to break out of routine can be beneficial if you play your cards right. This is not the time for false modesty. Assertiveness on your part is necessary. You can also take advantage of contacts with important people if you resolve to make an impression. Support and encouragement from friends and family can spur you on to do your best.

Financial affairs could go well this week. It is a good time to put some of your moneymaking ideas into effect. Transactions you complete now can result in an improvement in personal and family prosperity.

Home projects may be at the top of your to-do list. If you have a desire to try out a new hobby, now can be the time. You will be surprised at how relaxing it can be. You can find that you really enjoy it. Some of you Capricorns get so caught up in your business, professional, or routine life that you forget to take time out for yourselves. This is a good time to do just so.

39th Week/September 24–30

Tuesday the 24th. You can reach an understanding with a child or a younger person. The accent now is on fun and things that bring you pleasure. A recital or other musical event is especially nice. Try to do something dramatic for an uplifting night. A concert, theater, or even dancing would be great. Shopping can be fun, but leave the credit cards at home.

Wednesday the 25th. Stand firm against appeals to sentiment. Some people around you are rushing to change things, without providing convincing evidence. Let the stubborn facts speak for themselves, not the stubborn associates. If you go shopping, you will want a combination of quality and style, and you are willing to pay handsomely for the best. Some excellent pieces purchased now will increase in value over the years.

Thursday the 26th. Don't assume anything at present. Read or listen carefully to instructions. It can be easier than other days to get confused and to lose your way with important details and paperwork. If you make a wrong turn when driving, you may end up in an unfamiliar neighborhood. This may not be a complete loss if you are in the mood to go exploring.

Friday the 27th. You're probably critical now of yourself as well as others. If you must confront someone, please do so with utmost care. It will be possible to make your point in a fair and considerate way if you take the time to rehearse first. Cleaning out drawers and closets can be an effective way of handling stress. Hobbies, especially constructive ones, can be most satisfying.

Saturday the 28th. Try not to let the cat out of the bag when it comes to a special surprise. Although it may be tempting, keep secrets to yourself. Your partner may be ultrasensitive, so use consideration when talking to him or her. Some folks are likely to be in need of a little extra attention and nurturing. A phone call can be a really nice gesture to one who is feeling low.

Sunday the 29th. A close relationship may be in focus now. Moving to the next level of commitment may be on your mind. This can mean taking on a new business partnership. Likewise, an existing one may be going through changes. A member of the opposite sex may have an offer you cannot refuse. Pick up the phone and place a call that is long overdue.

Monday the 30th. A situation at work may seem more difficult than it actually is. Your energy may be low, and you may not feel like doing a whole lot. If you're productive and work hard you will have something to be proud of. Don't butt heads with a partner, who is almost sure to win. You may need to discuss a financial issue with your spouse. Keep an open mind.

Weekly Summary

Personal and professional goals can be updated now. Start preparing for something big that you have been considering. A meeting with a vocational counselor or other consultant may prove extremely helpful. Spending time alone also is important. The idea is to get insight into the steps you need to take in order to have the life you want. Writing in a journal can be very helpful.

A difficult relationship probably is improving by now, especially if you are giving it your all. You are feeling more tolerant and compassionate. If you're feeling down, you may wish to sit down and count your blessings in order to put the situation into perspective. If you're going through major changes in your personal life, try to view it as an opportunity.

An insensitive person may bring up something from the past, affecting you more than you thought possible. It would be wise to learn from your mistakes and get on with it. Dwelling on something you cannot change will not do you any good. Harsh words can be regretted. Be prepared for the possibility of unexpected house guests this week.

40th Week/October 1–7

Tuesday October 1st. Someone close to you may really need your help, attention, or sympathy. It's likely that your efforts will make all the difference. Offer to run errands, do chores, or assist financially. Those of you who are involved in a significant relationship may need to pay your partner extra heed. It cannot hurt to offer your loved one an extra hug or two.

Wednesday the 2nd. A situation involving money and legal issues may need your attention. An insurance settlement can require additional research before being finalized. If you have any doubt in your mind whatsoever, don't hesitate to hire a lawyer or other consultant for advice. Don't approach your boss for a raise if you can avoid it; wait a day or two instead.

Thursday the 3rd. You may see more people this day than usual. Expect more mail. The phone can be ringing off the hook. If the weather is nice, you will probably find the entire office sitting outside over the lunch break. A birthday party for a friend will be more fun than you imagine. You may have the opportunity to flirt with someone intriguing.

Friday the 4th. This will be an excellent day for business meetings. Your mind should be quite sharp. Your communication skills are highlighted too. Even telephone conferences and letter writing can be good. Complete tasks you may have put off. You will be glad you did. The focus this evening is on home. You may have a business dinner at your place.

Saturday the 5th. Possibly something at work is not up to par. You may not be properly organized. Now is the time to take care of such things before they get out of hand. Try to set aside some time to clean up a messy desk or files. If you need to have an important discussion with someone in regard to his or her job performance, go gently and with consideration.

Sunday the 6th. Don't let sensitivity get the better of you. You have a tendency to take things personally.

Negative people will leave you feeling especially drained and vulnerable. If this happens, you must realize that it is they, not you, who have a problem. Art or music can bring pleasure. You may enjoy a visit to a museum or library.

Monday the 7th. You may have to put your money where your mouth is, so to speak. Perhaps you have made a promise that you will have a hard time keeping. Luckily, you should be able to fix the problem easily enough. Confess your situation immediately and with sincerity. The other party should understand. Take care of any final details or organizing you need to attend to.

Weekly Summary

You will be able to count on people to give you a hand with whatever you need this week. If you need the assistance of someone, don't hesitate to call. Make sure you give credit where it's due. You will be glad you did. If you find yourself with a few spare moments this week, why not phone someone just to say hello? Be grateful for those whom you care about.

A legal matter can be resolved to your benefit this week. Extra work and research can help to sway matters your way. Consult with a lawyer or other professional if you have any doubts about your position. If you don't feel that things are going your way, don't give up hope. Perhaps you just need to approach things from a different angle.

Your luck will be better than usual at this time. Put your imagination to work for breakthrough ideas and problem solving. An unusual project shows financial promise. Don't allow this fantastic opportunity to slip away. It can really happen if you play your cards right.

Contact those who can help make the difference. A new or renewed partnership may be possible.

41st Week/October 8–14

Tuesday the 8th. Turn your attention toward a big project you may be planning. Take small steps toward getting it going. It can pay off more than you expect, if only in the satisfaction of a job well done. Group projects and ventures can be profitable. You can get the attention of someone who is in a position to help you out. Try not to take a playful remark the wrong way.

Wednesday the 9th. A group effort may be more challenging than you think. Working hard and staying focused can bring the results you are seeking. Other people need you to be optimistic right now. They trust your ideas and resourcefulness, and so should you. You may have to choose between romance and friendship tonight. Whatever you do should be fun.

Thursday the 10th. Listen carefully to the words of a friend. A seemingly incredible story may really be true. You may have a lesson to learn from someone else's mistake. Don't be quick to pass judgment or cast stones. This may now seem unimportant but soon will make a lot of sense. Pay back any favors at this time. A stranger you meet can be very interesting if you pay attention.

Friday the 11th. Your dreams can provide some important insight at this time. Write them down, then try to understand what they mean. What are they trying to tell you? Meditation and contemplation also are very important methods of gaining perspective. Watch for strong emotions tonight. Try to get your point of view across in a gentle but firm manner.

Saturday the 12th. Can you keep a secret? Avoid a temptation to spill the beans. Your promise to a friend is more important. Do what you need to do but from behind the scenes. Sometimes it's more effective that way. Stretch your imagination. Enjoy a book or movie that's pure escape. Spend some time doing something you really, truly enjoy.

Sunday the 13th. Your mood can be contagious, so make it a good one. Family members can be quite sensitive, so try to have a good attitude. Your charity can really help out in your community. You may feel very generous and bighearted. Helping another can benefit your own personal plans. Try not to promise more than you can deliver lest you disappoint yourself as well as someone else.

Monday the 14th. Pay some heed to your appearance now. If it has been more than a few years since you changed your hairstyle, this is the time to do so. Make an appointment with a stylist and ask for his or her opinion about what would be a good look for you. Health is in focus now as well, and you may want to consider adding an exercise program to your agenda.

Weekly Summary

You probably will need to do some repairs at this time. Try not to put it off. To do so might make matters worse. You may want to hire a professional to help you out. If you do, make sure you get at least three estimates lest you end up spending far more than you need to. Likewise, hire someone reputable and check references.

An older person may challenge you this week. Or you may be asked to mediate between two sides. Either way you are the one who has to be peacemaker. Being fair and reasonable should remedy the situation. Make sure you are being fair to yourself, however. This is not a situation where you should sacrifice truthfulness and honesty just for the sake of peace.

Follow up on business started last week. A phone call you receive at work will prove quite enlightening. A secretary or clerk may have some useful and interesting information for you. Try to answer and return all messages this week. Being a perfectionist is not realistic right now. Be easy on yourself. Avoid too much caffeine. You can easily get nervous and jittery.

42nd Week/October 15–21

Tuesday the 15th. A modest gain in speculation or a risky venture is very possible. Play by the rules and don't get discouraged. Your best luck and good fortune can come from your highly ethical and truthful action. Solitude is favored. Sing in the shower or write a poem. Enjoy your own wonderful company. Don't believe everything you see and hear on television or radio.

Wednesday the 16th. Consider allowing yourself to make that big purchase you may have been thinking about. Your partner will be very supportive. Social events may be on the schedule and will probably go off without a hitch. Last-minute plans for parties or dinners can be a really good idea. Try to let loose and have some fun. Romantic dates are possible.

Thursday the 17th. You may have an opportunity to make a positive career move. Something you have read recently can show you the way. You are likely to be restless and ready for action. Your charm and magnetism work well to convince others of your ideas. Be bold and courageous. People will be attracted by your enthusiasm. Meet a friend for lunch if you can.

Friday the 18th. Siblings and neighbors are featured. People seem to enjoy a good joke or two. There is a slight danger of folks being stubborn and argumentative, but that should pass soon enough. If you see this happening, you can change the subject quickly or exit the room gracefully. Obey all traffic and safety rules at this time. You may get a ticket if you don't.

Saturday the 19th. Expect the unexpected with a family member. The surprise will probably be a positive or happy one. You can be lucky when it comes to money, but you shouldn't bet the farm. Keep yourself busy this evening with socializing or spending time with loved ones. Your mind will be very sharp. This can be a great time to do something creative or artistic.

Sunday the 20th. Spend some time getting your household in order if you can. The next week or so promises to be quite busy, and this may be your last chance to take care of such things. Nervous tension can make you feel ill. If you have someone to pamper you, take advantage and let yourself relax and be waited on. If not, you can treat yourself. Allow yourself some rest this evening.

Monday the 21st. Do take a break if you have been working too hard. You may be left feeling exhausted if you don't. Focus is on the family, your mom and dad, or your role as a parent. For some of you, your friends are those whom you're closest to. Don't forget about them. You can feel psychic around these people. Your intuition is trying to tell you something; pay close attention.

Weekly Summary

Some of you haven't been taking care of yourselves properly. If this applies to you, now is the time to do something about it. You can begin a new exercise routine such as running, lifting weights, or yoga. Just make sure to get the approval of your physician, especially if you are aware of having any previous health problems. Simple things like drinking more water can make a difference.

If you have kids, you may find some unusual and exciting activity to share with them. A visit to a science center, forest, or farm may be just the thing to stretch their imaginations while having fun. While you're at it, make sure you take some time out this week for some pleasure time yourself. Art, music, and movies can be fantastic, especially if you see them with someone special.

People find you very attractive right now. A new romance may already be starting. Be open to the possibility of developing a romance with someone with whom you are already friends. However, being overly flirtatious can get you into hot water. You can attract someone in whom you aren't really interested and have to pick up the pieces later.

43rd Week/October 22–28

Tuesday the 22nd. Someone from your past may show up unexpectedly. You don't have to begin a relationship again if you don't want to. Go ahead and feel confident about yourself when it comes to a certain job situation. Stand your ground and don't shy away if you're concerned about the competition. It may be productive to have dinner with a business associate tonight.

Wednesday the 23rd. This is not the day for procrastination. A simple trip across town may not be as easy as it sounds. Delays are likely. Allow extra time for traffic. Maintaining cars and other vehicles is always a good idea. Simple things like oil changes and tune-ups can make a big difference. Return an important phone call early in the day rather than later.

Thursday the 24th. The day offers an excellent opportunity for romance. Somebody you met recently is very charming. If you are interested, and available, this can be a good connection. If not, make plans to spend time with your significant other. An art gallery or beautiful park can be magical. Channel excess energy through exercise. Use caution when driving heavy machinery. Obey safety rules.

Friday the 25th. If you have taken on more than you can comfortably handle lately, you may need to make some changes. Don't hesitate when it comes to delegating some of your work to others. Let others help out more with household chores. You may even consider hiring someone so you can focus on the work that is most important to you. Try not to let a news story affect you.

Saturday the 26th. Give yourself a pat on the back for a job well done. This can be a very lucky day in love and money. Your charm and magnetism attracts others. You are popular and well-liked, especially at work or in public. You should have success working with children or anything creative. It's a better day than most for making a presentation.

Sunday the 27th. A special relationship can be rewarding. A new romance may have more potential than you think. You may be attracted to someone from work. If this is the case, give it lots of thought. You do not want to get caught up in office gossip. Otherwise, people should be friendly and helpful. Enter into a new contract with caution.

Monday the 28th. You may find yourself asked to take sides. Try not to sit on the fence. Do try to think your words through before speaking in this regard, however, especially if the two parties involved are important to you. People can be a bit standoffish, so don't take it too personally if you encounter such a person. A unique idea can come to you. Dare to be a bit different.

Weekly Summary

You may feel as though you're spinning your wheels this week, as people or issues put a damper on your ambitions. You will get frustrated if you can't relax about it. Focus on the important things and let the details fall into place. If you're planning a social event, you may get uptight if things don't seem to be going exactly as you would like. Folks will not care about the little details, so don't worry.

You will need to think your words through before you speak, especially toward the end of the week. You do have a tendency to speak without thinking. People can be awfully opinionated and may not want to listen to what you have to say. Avoid discussions involving controversial subjects. Try to be as positive and considerate as possible if you have to give constructive criticism or advice.

Your desires can be high where love it concerned, but circumstances may not be on your side. Relationships can feel intense, or can have some difficult moments. Don't let this stop you from showing someone your interest, however. You can always pick up where you left off and go from there. Besides, absence really can make the heart grow fonder.

44th Week/October 29–November 4

Tuesday the 29th. Partnership issues can come up now. You may be able to get something out in the open that has been bugging you. People will be warm and open to communicating about things they ordinarily might find difficult to talk about. You may be setting up an equal business partnership. This is an excellent day to run through the details and set limits.

Wednesday the 30th. Try not to make important financial decisions if you can avoid it, especially if other people and their money are involved. Taking risks may not work out as planned. Any action taken should be as conservative as possible. Your security may depend on it. Spend time with family this evening. Be diplomatic but firm when dealing with younger folks.

Thursday the 31st. Sudden changes in plans may catch you by surprise. Try to be as flexible as you can. Keep your eyes and ears open for new ideas. Take care of any outstanding debts. Money you owe to other people has a way of incurring interest faster than you realize. A major purchase may involve a cosigner or joint investment. Don't let the cat out of the bag.

Friday November 1st. Try to be conscious of time. It can be all too easy to lose track and find yourself late. Double-check your work if you have a deadline. You may need to become more disciplined. Take some time out for reflection if you can, but only after you have taken care of business. Make sure you are well dressed and groomed. You never know whom you will meet.

Saturday the 2nd. It will be nice if you can take some time to get away from it all. If you have been working hard, you should be experiencing progress and will probably benefit from taking a break. Take some time to reflect on how your personal philosophies in life may have led you to where you are now. Take time out to make a phone call to a friend.

Sunday the 3rd. Give some thought to the week ahead. What would you like to accomplish? Your mind is sharp, and you have many good ideas. Write them down for later use. This can be a good time to expand into new areas and skills. Team sports or other competitions may do you a world of good. In fact, any physical exercise is excellent for you now.

Monday the 4th. Whatever you do, give it your all. Someone who is in a position to give you a raise or promotion may be watching. Listen to what your friends have to say about a relationship or partnership. They may see something you don't. It's probably no big deal, but some adjustment may be called for. There's no reason why you shouldn't invite someone over tonight.

Weekly Summary

Holiday planning will be on your mind. You may be torn between choices of visiting family or staying home. If you're hoping to travel by plane, train, or bus, make sure you have your ticket booked already, before it is too late. If you are planning a trip to a foreign country, get started immediately on passports and any other things you need to arrange.

The beginning of this week can be advantageous for gathering new information useful at work or in your studies. You may find yourself heading into two lines of thinking, especially if you are looking to expand your reputation in area of career. This week you are able to manage more than one thing at a time. You may find yourself signing up for a course.

You may be invited to attend or even plan a party. This can be a great time for socializing, so go ahead and put your full effort into it. People are chatty and humorous. You may even want to revise age-old party games such as charades. Why not look up an old friend or two whom you haven't seen in ages? You can have a pleasant surprise waiting for you.

45th Week/November 5–11

Tuesday the 5th. You can experience good luck in business and should feel blessed with abundance. A professional association or group may hold the key. Your dreams, both day and night, can be significant sources of inspiration. Get yourself outdoors and enjoy the fresh air. It can make you feel energetic and enthusiastic. Engage in sports if possible. Be sure to vote; it could be a close regional election.

Wednesday the 6th. Teamwork is probably the best way to go, both at work and at play. You can benefit from the multitalents of good colleagues around you. The atmosphere can be fun-filled. It may be inspiring to share stories about the good old days with school chums. All legal dealings are highly favored. Renewed contracts can be very good news.

Thursday the 7th. If you don't have to work, attending an afternoon movie can be a pleasant way to pass the day lazily. You may bump into a friend you haven't seen for ages. You may be quite surprised to see how much he or she has changed. A walk through the park can be quite entertaining. Watching people should be fun. Strangers may seem particularly odd or interesting to watch.

Friday the 8th. Don't be too quick to say yes to a friend who is offering you a chance to make easy money. The idea you are presented with may be riskier than you are being told. Don't forget to pay attention to the time on your parking meter. Better to add a few extra coins in order to avoid worrying about getting a ticket. Treat your elders with the respect they deserve.

Saturday the 9th. Your partner may be in a more romantic mood than you are. Perhaps you are making plans for a social night with the gang, while he or she is hoping to find time alone with you. Be aware of the subtle signals that are put out, or you will wonder later why your loved one has hurt feelings. A little gift can be a delightful surprise to someone who isn't expecting it.

Sunday the 10th. Perhaps you will feel better off in solitude. When left to your own devices, you are likely to be very productive. Turn some favorite music on for company. You may be amazed at how resourceful you can be when needing to find an unusual object or service. Writing in a journal can help you to solve a problem. Putting things down on paper can be a big help.

Monday the 11th. This can be a very busy day indeed. You probably will pick up extra responsibilities on the job. Relationships can be demanding too. With so many things happening at once, you may lose track of important details. It is wise to keep a list of priorities and stick to them, as interruptions can make life confusing. You may want to take the phone off the hook.

Weekly Summary

You may be feeling driven to accomplish career goals. Competition can help to spur you forward. However, keeping your own true focus will most likely be the best route. Knowing your limits is important. Allow yourself to reach one goal before setting another. You may need to examine your motives in this area. Think more about doing what you love.

Stress from work or the home situation can drain your physical energy unless you make a conscious effort to relax and let go. Exercise can be very helpful, but you may need to see a counselor or have a good, long talk with a trusted friend in order to release pent-up emotions. Tension-releasing exercises such as yoga, tai-chi, or martial arts can be very helpful.

Spiritual pursuits will be on the minds of some of you. This is an excellent time for some serious meditation, contemplation, and prayer. If you have ever thought about doing these things, this week will be a great time to start doing so. There are many types of spiritual groups that are more than willing to share their ideas with you. Try a local community resource guide for a start.

46th Week/November 12–18

Tuesday the 12th. You may be surprised by an unexpected check or other financial reward. If no such thing is forthcoming, you may still have a chance to improve your earning situation. Becoming better educated may be one way. Perhaps you can read one book that will make you a better employee or businessperson. You may soon be traveling in relation to your work.

Wednesday the 13th. You seem to be attracted to luxurious things now, and you may be tempted to spoil yourself. You will feel better at the end of the day if you have made wise purchases, however. Keep this in mind if you are out shopping. Stress and tension may lead to overeating. Those of you who are watching your weight may want to keep that in mind.

Thursday the 14th. It may be time to take the car for maintenance or troubleshooting. Get a tune-up if you haven't done so for a while. Take your time with any elaborate or complicated paperwork. If you slow down, you will be more likely to get through difficult accounting with ease. Eat healthy food and drink plenty of water in order to keep your energy pumped up.

Friday the 15th. You can finish old business, much to your relief. Clearing the clutter out of your life allows wonderful new changes to come in. Take a few minutes out for refreshment. A younger co-worker can be fun to take a break with. A change of routine can be relaxing. Your time and care with a complicated situation involving a friend may save the day.

Saturday the 16th. Folks should be upbeat and optimistic now. Make plans to hang out with those you care about the most. You're likely to be the star of the show. When spending time with loved ones, be generous. Allow yourself to reach and dream big. Your fascination with a certain stranger can lead to something bigger. You just never know what will happen.

Sunday the 17th. Try to spend some quality time with a loved one. A heart-to-heart talk that is long overdue may be just what you need. A casual relationship may be turning into something a little more structured. Or a friendship can take a turn toward romance. Take it easy when it comes to criticizing the work of others. Tact and diplomacy can go a long way.

Monday the 18th. Many of you will want to stay home and make yourselves comfortable if you can. You may be more sensitive than usual now, and can take things too personally. If you find this is the case, try to discuss it gently, rather than run away and hide. Enjoy creature comforts like curling up on the couch with a good book. Stop worrying so much.

Weekly Summary

Your job may keep you busier than you expected. Issues at work can be challenging. An intense encounter with a co-worker will end well, however, if you show consideration for his or her feelings. Be on the lookout for new ideas to help make things run more smoothly. Your bank account should be responding well to any changes you made last month.

You may not agree with your spouse when it comes to dealing with a domestic issue this week. Make sure to tell your point of view, since you may have a tendency not to and then feel angry about it later. Excess energy can be put to use in doing home projects, cleaning up, or playing sports. Working with your loved ones side-by-side can be quite rewarding. Try not to overspend.

You can be lucky in love if you play your cards right. Your intuition is very strong now and works well where matters of the heart are concerned. Try to separate heart from head, and don't be afraid to follow your feelings. Expect the unusual, exciting, and unexpected. Be open to new ideas and people. You never know what kind of adventure you might have.

47th Week/November 19–25

Tuesday the 19th. You may be inspired to do some home decorating or interior design. If you don't feel confident about your own talents for design, copy someone else's. Creativity can really flow, so those of you who are artists may want to take some time to do a project. People at home can be ultrasensitive now, so be careful of their feelings. A nice quiet evening may be just the ticket.

Wednesday the 20th. A young person may be trying to get in contact with you. You can be of great service here. Your ethical behavior sets a good example. A situation that once seemed impossible now seems more likely. Don't hesitate to ask an important question. It can be more important than you think. You may get a pleasant surprise in the mail.

Thursday the 21st. Like it or not, you may have to work or do some unpleasant chores. Your attitude makes all the difference in how the day goes. Singing or listening to music can help to pass the time. You may even have fun. Those of you who are single can be hit with one of Cupid's arrows at a social event or through a group. Be open to the possibilities.

Friday the 22nd. Your job may be more demanding than usual. Keep your nose to the grindstone, and you should get ahead. Your boss is likely appreciate any effort you make to get a project finished before deadline. Do-it-yourself projects can fun and satisfying. Pay attention to any domestic matters you may have put off. Family should be a priority at this time.

Saturday the 23rd. It's a great day to get some exercise. A long walk in the woods can be ideal. If not, try racket sports with a friend with whom you enjoy competing. Watch the time if you are speaking on the phone long-distance. You can run up quite a bill if you aren't paying attention. Going dancing tonight can be fun. Bring along a friend who is feeling lonely.

Sunday the 24th. Someone you love is surely overdue for some pampering today. Showering your significant other with gifts may not be out of the question. If you've been in the doghouse lately, it would be an especially nice gesture. Shopping will be therapeutic if you have been stressed out lately. A touchy situation this evening requires your utmost patience and calm.

Monday the 25th. Good communication with a romantic partner or business associate is necessary today. Emotional extremes and overreactions are possible. Try to find a balance between your own needs and the needs of others. You will get your message across in the end. A perfect resolution is probable. Invite a close relative to join you for dinner. Entertaining at home is favored.

Weekly Summary

You will be feeling highly motivated at work now, perhaps more so then the people around you. If you are ready to get moving on a project, but others are not, examine your motives. Could it be that you are jumping the gun a little? This is only one possibilty. Perhaps others are lagging behind. Either way you'll have to identify the problem before you solve it.

This is an excellent time to break an old habit, especially one that affects your physical or mental health. Daily routines can be transformed for the good. As the job changes, you will experience positive feelings. Take control of your future by careful planning. You're more optimistic than usual now, so use it to your advantage. A parent is willing to help out.

A tiff with a significant other is likely to be just that. While relationships are in focus over the next month or so, this event should blow over quickly. At the root of the issue my be your own need to have everything perfect. By the end of the week you should be seeing things clearly and can easily move forward in romance.

48th Week/November 26–December 2

Tuesday the 26th. Joint financial issues may appear during this time. It can be that you and a loved one are at odds about what to do with an investment. Insurance can also be an issue now. You would probably be better off to take out extra coverage than to try to cut back. Talk to an expert if you are at all unsure. Romance can be deeply fulfilling now and for the next day or so.

Wednesday the 27th. A friend's suggestion can be key to helping you solve a sticky situation involving your significant other. Allow yourself to communicate your feelings, especially when it comes to relationships. Consider the points of view of others, even if they are significantly different from your own. If you have indecision about whether to go out or stay at home tonight, let someone else decide.

Thursday the 28th. You may have to put the needs of another before your own this Thanksgiving Day. Your compassion can be just what the situation calls for although you may not like it that much. Travel plans may be on the agenda. Allow extra time for all trips and double-check arrival and departure times. Dealing with difficult people requires your patience and understanding.

Friday the 29th. A scheduled trip may turn out to be more than you have planned on. Make sure you leave early if you have to get to the airport. Expect the unexpected at work. Keep on your toes, as you may be in for a surprise. An eccentric idea to which you haven't given much thought can become important. In romance, sparks may fly.

Saturday the 30th. A partner may not see eye-to-eye with you when it comes to your goals. He or she may have a point, however. You have to compromise. Rest assured, in the end you will make the right choice. Get an agreement in writing if you need to. Physical activity is energizing, especially if you feel tired. Hanukkah activities can enchant a special child.

Sunday December 1st. People will be quick to recognize you now. Your willingness to go the extra mile can make all the difference in the world. You may finally come to agreement on a big deal you have wanted for a long time. Having an important person over for dinner will make a good impression. Burn off aggression or excess energy through exercise or competition.

Monday the 2nd. You should be feeling lucky. Your confidence level is higher than usual. Relax, and allow your charm to come out. Being around others can be a real boost. Enthusiasm can get results. Everyone is a star in one way or another. Allow your own star to shine through. Single Capricorns may have a chance for love. Don't be timid, or you may miss out.

Weekly Summary

This is the time to make an assessment of what does and does not work when it comes to your job or career. A practical approach may work best for you. Let go of ideas that aren't working for you, and focus more on the ones that are. If you have considered returning to school, this is a great time to start making plans. Sit down with pen and paper and write out all of your talents, desires, and challenges.

You single Capricorns should be on the lookout for a new romantic interest to come into your life. If you want to get involved, now is the time to get yourself out there. Groups and associations can be a good bet. Be aware, however, that you may send signals to the wrong person if you're not careful. Save your charm for those with whom you are serious.

Physically, you may be stressed or experience tension. This can have to do with worries or anger. It is very important that you do some relaxation exercises in this case. Some of you will find that you are working far too much for too little reward. If so, think about how you can change all that. If you feel you have been penned up indoors, try to get out and take a long walk or go to the gym.

49th Week/December 3–9

Tuesday the 3rd. Prepare yourself for opportunity. You may find the courage to ask for what you really want. Just be sure you want it. A female, perhaps much older, is willing to help you when you least expect it. Watch that you communicate clearly, especially when using electronic media. Don't leave out any facts. Try not to let others speak for you.

Wednesday the 4th. You have all the energy you need now. However, if your career aspirations are taking up too much of your time, take a break. A significant other may not appreciate all the extra time you have been devoting to your work. Avoid arguments; they can get out of control. If you are single, you may find yourself attracted to a dark-haired person.

Thursday the 5th. You should have the initiative necessary to get started on a new project. This is a most auspicious time to do so unless you are the type of person who starts things without finishing current ones. In that case, you would be wise to devote your energy to completing your original deal. Turn on your inner spark and allow your light to shine.

Friday the 6th. You may find yourself daydreaming more than usual. To use this time productively, listen to your intuition. Gather all the facts you need in order to make a good decision. It may be difficult to tell the difference between right and wrong. Speak very clearly lest someone misunderstand you. Your night dreams can be very revealing.

Saturday the 7th. You may be feeling more optimistic than usual. Make sure, however, that in your good mood you remain sensitive to the feelings of others. It is all too easy to open your mouth and stick your foot in it. This just may be one of those days when it's better to observe quietly than to comment. Have patience when it comes to exuberant children.

Sunday the 8th. Keep your eyes open and your feet on the ground. You may be a bit in the clouds, likely to be taken for a ride or even to lose things. Pay attention to all warning signs and precautions, particularly when driving. You may be tempted to take chances. If that is the case, think it through first. Take some time out for your own pleasure and relaxation.

Monday the 9th. Start a savings account if possible, even if it's only a jar of coins. It will do very well indeed. This is a good time for self-improvement of all kinds. Take your exercise habits into account. This is an excellent time to start or revise a healthy habit. Why not order some Christmas gifts by mail? You can find yourself the life of the party this evening.

Weekly Summary

You may be way overdue for a change as far as your appearance is concerned. This week is a good time to do what's necessary to update your image. Some of you may be needing a more professional style. Take a trusted friend shopping with you to get a good opinion. Don't rely on the sales clerk for that. Then don't forget to take your friend out for a nice meal or a cup of coffee to show your thanks.

The major focus this week is on friends and associates. Networking has never been easier and more effective for you than now. Use the latest technology to keep in touch with contacts. Don't get left behind when it comes to new gadgets. You may feel shy in a social situation, but you will get over it soon enough. Don't be afraid to laugh at yourself.

You will have lots of extra energy to devote to a new moneymaking opportunity or part-time job. You can start bringing in some extra dough. If you're interested in turning a hobby into a cash cow, go to the library and read up on some entrepreneurs who have done just that. Don't quit your day job, however, until you start seeing some results.

50th Week/December 10–16

Tuesday the 10th. Spend the morning catching up on old business. Be sure to answer all of your calls and return all messages. Your sales and marketing skills are admirable right now. Buying and selling is quite favorable. Hold out for your best possible price. You may even do well on a speculation if you try your luck. Home entertaining this evening is a definite plus.

Wednesday the 11th. Money matters can come to the fore. It's possible you are worrying more than you need to. On the one hand, concerns may be realistic, and you shouldn't ignore them. On the other hand, try not to make to make mountains out of molehills. You may be tempted to buy something you don't need and cannot afford. Avoid the malls if you are the type of person who overspends.

Thursday the 12th. Focus on communications and relating to others. This can be an excellent time to write and edit papers or make phone calls. You may find yourself quite busy on the phone all day. Lunch with a co-worker can be quite interesting. A potential concern with your boss will turn out to be no big deal. Enjoy a social event or night on the town, but don't overdo it.

Friday the 13th. Your original ideas can help you at work or school. Charisma can really get you noticed. Sales can be excellent if you turn on the charm. A friendship may be turning into more than just a platonic thing. Married couples will get a chance to rekindle the flame this evening. Why not plan a special date, dress up, and go out to dinner and dancing?

Saturday the 14th. Home projects can be fun and go by quickly if you have a work party. You can invite friends and supply the food and refreshments. Offer to do the same for them one day. You should be in the mood for doing something fun and out of the ordinary at this time. Romance is more than likely. Don't hesitate to be the one to initiate a conversation or ask for a date.

Sunday the 15th. Home and family life may need extra care at this time. Children will be a handful, to say the least. Distraction may be the best way to handle a tantrum. Loving relationships can grow through mutual respect, nurturing, and support. Thoughtfulness, consideration, and loving, kind words of encouragement can produce the most remarkable results.

Monday the 16th. Socializing at home or at the home of a good friend may be just the thing to do. People will be gracious and considerate, making for some pleasant times. Enjoy good conversations, artistic endeavors. You can be honest with a relative about a touchy subject. Just approach him or her with kindness and respect. Romance is possible in the evening hours.

Weekly Summary

Continue ongoing projects to aid your career advancement and financial gain. You may need to take a good look at your budget and make sure you're not overspending. Sound investments can pay off. Clearing old debts can free your energy to do more creative things. You may want to start a new savings account or contribute to a retirement or education fund.

Try to accept all social invitations and proposals. You can be in for an exciting week when it comes to meeting new people. All things are possible. New contacts for business can be made. You never know who knows whom. The more friends you have, the more potential there is for success. An intriguing stranger catches your eye, but things may not be what they seem.

Brothers and sisters, cousins, and family affairs are featured this week. You may be involved in planning a family gathering. Why not see how many people you can invite for a nice dinner or other get-together? Your sense of humor can help a relative to see a difficult situation in a brighter light. Your devotion to your family makes you a good role model.

51st Week/December 17–23

Tuesday the 17th. A supervisor or boss can be helpful if you allow it. Extra time and effort you spend at work are not likely to go without notice. A child may be a handful now. You will get better results with the youngster if you stop and take a deep breath. A creative project may be stalled but should pick up shortly. Have patience. Think about having a medical checkup if you are due for one.

Wednesday the 18th. You may have to put your foot down with children. Parenting can take extra effort now. Although it is simpler to give in to their requests, let them earn their rewards. Offer them something they want only after they do their chores. Work as fast as possible on any mindless jobs, and you can end up with extra time to read or watch some television.

Thursday the 19th. You may feel frustrated because you have so many things to do. If you're overwhelmed by it all, take a breather. Write down a list of priorities and check them off one by one. Don't be hard on yourself, either. You have a way of being overly self-critical. On the other hand, you can complete an important job or at least make some headway.

Friday the 20th. You may solve an important problem. Approach troubleshooting from a new perspective. Original ideas may get you recognized. You can learn a lot by teaching another. Important projects can crystallize from across the miles, perhaps even internationally. More assertive sales techniques will get results. Get some exercise if at all possible.

Saturday the 21st. You may be insensitive to the feelings of another without even being aware of it. Through no fault of your own, people can be more vulnerable than usual. You will need to be very cautious when giving criticism. A mystery that involves two friends can be brought to light. Working in a group can be challenging, rewarding, and exhausting.

Sunday the 22nd. The holiday season reminds us to cherish those we love. Try to spend some quality time with your spouse if you are married. Some of you will be turning your thoughts toward charity at this time. There are lots of ways to help those who are more disadvantaged than you. Food banks need donations this time of year. Perhaps you can help out a friend too.

Monday the 23rd. Get prepared for the busy times ahead. Take care of minor details so you can relax and have some fun. Something you have been putting off can come back to haunt you if you don't clear it out of the way. Working with your hands is favored. Some of you may be planning to do some big projects. Work the details out on paper before you start.

Weekly Summary

You may find that you're ahead of the game financially. You can get an unexpected windfall. Be careful, however, that you don't spend the money faster than it comes in. Another option is that you may save so much money that it feels as though you have actually made some. You may be able to find some amazing bargains if you look carefully. But try not to be cheap.

Work can feel a bit overwhelming at this time. You seem to have lots of extra duties and responsibilities. Try to pass a few of these off to some others in the workplace who may not be pulling their weight. Your frustrations and focus on perfection can cause you to be overcritical. Try not to let that happen, or you may be stuck with an unhappy co-worker.

Your health should be an area of focus this week. If you are sensitive to stress, foods, or environmental factors, you may want to take extra precautions. Eating lots of sugars and fats cannot be good for you, no matter how many people are offering them to you. Remember, everything in moderation. Make sure you take some time out of your busy schedule to go for a nice, vigorous walk.

52nd Week/December 24–31

Tuesday the 24th. Focus is on partnerships and friendships. You may have to calm down a loved one who is feeling stressed out. People have a way of getting melancholy during the holidays, so offer your shoulder and a nice hug. If you have guests, make sure they don't drink and drive. If you haven't already planned tomorrow's menu, why not try something new?

Wednesday the 25th. Merry Christmas! Allow this day to be relaxing. Although your instincts may tell you to work, work, work, fight them, at least for a little while. If you can allow yourself to take it easy, you will be better off for it. Allow others to help out in as many ways as possible. Let yourself get sentimental too. Sometimes you Capricorns get too focused on getting things done. Enjoy the moment.

Thursday the 26th. Impulse shopping is probably not a good idea. You may have to examine the reasons why you desire certain things. If you're just trying to keep up with the pack, think again. People can be somewhat unreliable. A family member may have a surprise this evening, and it may or may not be a pleasant one. Try to react in a positive way, however.

Friday the 27th. Try not to argue with others over issues like religion or politics. People can be highly opinionated and get on each other's nerves. You don't have to play those games, however. Just keep quiet, be polite, and listen. You can always laugh about it later. Spend some time reading a good book if you get a chance. Either that, or rent an epic film, just for fun.

Saturday the 28th. You will find that most people are in a good mood. Travelers should experience smooth journeys. If you meet someone who is grumpy or seems to be having a bad day, a small gesture can go far to improve his or her attitude. You may have a hard time making a decision. If so, go with the choice that seems more fun or more out of character for you.

Sunday the 29th. Romance is on your plate now. One of two things may happen. Either your romantic intentions may be dashed by the object of your affections, or you will have a too-good-to-be-true encounter. It's feast or famine at this time. Some of you have hunkered down to get back on track as far as work goes, but try to play a bit longer, if just for today.

Monday the 30th. If you're feeling preoccupied with career and moneymaking issues, it is probably a good thing. This is always a powerful time of the year for Capricorn folks, and you should use this to your advantage. Try to develop a game plan with some short- and long-term goals, to get you closer to where you would really like to be. On the job, people may not be too helpful.

Tuesday the 31st. As far as New Year's Eve parties are concerned, you can have a wonderful time at one this year. At the very least, you should try to mark the event by being with good friends and loved ones. You may be feeling more social than usual. Perhaps you will decide to throw a party yourself. Whatever you do, loosen up, relax, and charm others with that awesome Capricorn sense of humor.

Weekly Summary

If you have been avoiding speaking to a family member, this can be the perfect time to try to patch things up. Can you try to look at things from the other person's perspective? Perhaps you were a bit hasty in passing judgment, or came to a snap conclusion. If you can detach yourself from emotion and look at things logically, you may find a new perspective.

Staying at home is especially appealing now. You would rather be there than anywhere else in the world. Don't feel guilty if you want to take a few days off from work. You may just need some relaxation. Creative projects will go well. Religion and spirituality can be at the top of your list. You can be an inspiration to a family member. Take that role seriously.

Allow yourself to have a little more fun than usual. You may meet exciting new people. Your attitude will have a great deal to do with how you deal with an unexpected situation at work. You seem to be quite stubborn now. You may have to be flexible with your plans this week, as friends and family may have other ideas. Enjoy some luxury, however minor.

DAILY FORECASTS:
JULY–DECEMBER 2001

Sunday July 1st. This can be a great day for entertaining. Expect a friend's sense of humor to be quirky or even sarcastic. You may not like everything that's said in a group situation, but you don't need to respond. Give your partner the attention he or she needs.

Monday the 2nd. You may discover that a friend has been hiding something from you. Try not to overreact. He or she may have your best interest at heart. Think about what you can learn from a difficult situation. Consider how you can change things.

Tuesday the 3rd. Dreams can be more vivid than usual now. If you can remember what you dreamed about, give it some thought. It may help you to solve a problem or give you inspiration. You may feel like getting away from people this evening, and that's just fine.

Wednesday the 4th. If you haven't taken care of things lately, you can start catching up, even though it is a major holiday. List your chores, then do them one by one. Then you will feel free to watch a parade, have a picnic or party, or go to a concert.

Thursday the 5th. The spotlight is on personal appearance and personality. How another sees you may be less important than how you see yourself. If negotiating, silence can be your best weapon. Let the other person make the first offer, then go from there.

Friday the 6th. Pay close attention to what you're doing, especially with facts and figures. You can easily make a math error or get your data mixed up. Daydreaming can be positive, so take time out to let your thoughts wander. Your keys or small items are easy to lose.

Saturday the 7th. You may get a brilliant idea or two that helps you with your job. Make sure to write it down. Otherwise you can forget and lose it forever. If you have to work or do routine chores, try to figure out a new way of doing things. You will be bored easily. Listening to the radio can help.

Sunday the 8th. Try not to spend money unnecessarily. You may be tempted by a luxury that you don't need and cannot afford. On the other hand, you will want to allow yourself some reward for the hard work you have done. Just keep it in perspective. Excitement appeals now. Fast-paced sports can do the trick.

Monday the 9th. If you go shopping for something that makes you feel good, keep your loved ones in mind too. Someone close to you may have a birthday or other special day coming up. A charity organization you supported in the past may call on you again.

Tuesday the 10th. Try not to make an issue with a sibling more complicated than it is. Honest communication can clear it up. Pay bills on time, or you will hear from a creditor. You may not agree with your significant other over how to spend money.

Wednesday the 11th. You will be able to achieve some great things if you stick to your plan. Hard work can be its own reward. Take advantage of an opportunity to save money, one that may be worth more than you initially think. It's important to have a plan to follow. There's a chance of messing things up if you don't. Listen to the advice of a parent or older person.

Thursday the 12th. You're likely to have an uncanny ability to control your environment in a positive way. You can change someone's mood from bad to good with a smile. Being kind and generous has a way of coming back to you. You may win a contest. Charming manners help you climb the social ladder.

Friday the 13th. People can be self-directed now. Actions speak louder than words, so pay close attention to what is going on around you. Listen to what a brother or sister has to say. Some information may be true. Don't accept everything you hear at face value, but try to find some thread of truth.

Saturday the 14th. Family and relatives must take priority now. One of them may be facing a tough situation. You may have experienced something similar in the past, so you can be of great help to him or her. You may learn from a family member's mistake.

Sunday the 15th. You may be asking too much of yourself now. You will be better off to give yourself a break. Don't be too disappointed if you cannot always live up to the expectations of others. You may be overdue for some real rest. Solitary relaxation can take the pressure off. Cleaning up can be therapeutic.

Monday the 16th. An adjustment in your domestic or living situation may be under way. Frustrations are likely but may be necessary in order to bring about needed change. A sudden inspiration can provide the answer you're looking for. Don't dismiss what may seem like a wild idea. Get some exercise.

Tuesday the 17th. You may have to count way past ten to restore your calm and patience. If circumstances are out of your control, try to relax. People can be selfish or even mean at present, so try not to take it personally. A child may try your patience. Take the time to set a good example in a firm yet loving manner.

Wednesday the 18th. Taking care of details is likely to be satisfying. This will be an ideal time to make a friendly gesture. A caring act can lead to a closer bond with someone of whom you are merely an acquaintance. Health can be a concern now, so watch what you eat and drink. Allergic reactions are possible.

Thursday the 19th. People can be really sensitive, so tread lightly. Difficulties can arise between you and a co-worker. You may not see eye-to-eye on an important issue. If you feel you cannot resolve the issue, it should be okay to let it go for a day or two. Romance is not likely to go as you were hoping.

Friday the 20th. A misunderstanding between you and your spouse may be clearing up. However, it may not be as easy as it sounds. The situation is likely to be delicate. Your honesty and compassion will smooth ruffled feathers. You will prefer a quiet evening with loved ones to a party this evening.

Saturday the 21st. A loved one may be waiting for you to make the first move. Getting together with a sibling will be enlightening. Take along some pictures if you would like to reminisce about the good old days. A creative approach to budgeting will make your dollars go further. Romance will be full of surprises.

Sunday the 22nd. Be flexible when it comes to keeping an agenda. You may decide to change your plans. You can be feeling guilty if you haven't been taking good care of your body. Start a new workout program. Make something fun so you will stick to it.

Monday the 23rd. When it comes to a relationship, reach out now to get what you want. As they say, the squeaky wheel gets the grease. You must let your wishes be known, however, or you will miss out. Home repairs may be necessary, as there can be a safety factor involved. Avoid mishap by taking care now.

Tuesday the 24th. A financial mystery will seem to come to light. Things aren't always the way they appear. You will do well to remember that. There is a slight chance of biting off more than you can chew. Make sure any large purchases you make are necessary. Partners come through for you now.

Wednesday the 25th. You will have a busy day. Those of you who are in school can benefit from being extra nice to your teachers. You may be asked to settle a disagreement between two people. Follow your instincts if you have a hard time making decisions.

Thursday the 26th. Those of you who have identified your special talents should be willing to share them. Folks will be receptive to your product or service. You can gain recognition that leads to a financial benefit later. Don't be shy when it comes to romance.

Friday the 27th. On the job, you may end up being the star of the show. Research and investigation will pay off big time. Don't just skim the surface, however. You will need to get to the bottom of the mystery before you hit pay dirt. A media appearance is possible.

Saturday the 28th. Disruptions can be downright frustrating. This is a good time to implement time-management techniques. If you haven't thought of this, you should. Prioritize your project; take care of the most important things first. Avoid procrastinating.

Sunday the 29th. Your point of view may not be the same as that of a loved one. Working together with friends can get a tough job finished faster than going it alone. Avoid such controversial subjects as religion or politics. Not everyone shares your beliefs.

Monday the 30th. There is a potential for a conflict in business. Although unpleasant, it can be transforming in the end. Losing your temper will not be productive. Relationships may be challenging. Bring important issues into the light to avoid resentment.

Tuesday the 31st. Gather all the facts before making an important career or job decision. More research may be needed before you come up with a solution. A spiritual event with your significant other can be inspirational and may bring the two of you closer.

Wednesday August 1st. Don't believe everything you hear. A message can be mixed up. Try not to participate in gossip. Others can tempt you to play along, but someone may get hurt. Avoid exaggeration. Something you say can come back to haunt you.

Thursday the 2nd. The borrowing and lending of money will end up being disappointing if you're not clear on the arrangements. Make a contract. Fragile objects may be at risk. If you must handle antiques or valuable things, handle them gently.

Friday the 3rd. A new project may be more involved than you originally believed. A plan can be changed on the job. It may be best to give in rather than fight it. A long-distance call can bring interesting news. Today's daydreams can be tomorrow's goals.

Saturday the 4th. Avoid indiscriminate spending. A new moneymaking idea can pay off. You may want to try something that is different from anything you have done before. You will not know if you can do it unless you try. Be firm about collecting unpaid debts.

Sunday the 5th. You may want to buy or make something nice that soothes your soul and spirit. Music and art are perfect examples. Pay attention to your intuition in regard to your finances. Get advice if you're having difficulty understanding a relationship.

Monday the 6th. The spotlight is likely to be on financial affairs. You may not agree with your spouse on a money issue. Make an attempt to straighten things out. Standing up for yourself will not be easy, but it will be more than worth it. Follow your intuition.

Tuesday the 7th. Sometimes fixing someone's problem is not really the best solution for that person. You can be supportive without taking full responsibility. Spend time with your parents in person or on the phone. Don't hesitate to ask a neighbor for help.

Wednesday the 8th. A trip across town may not be as easy as it sounds. Delays are likely. Allow extra time for traffic. Checking out cars and other vehicles may be a good idea now. You should return an important phone call early in the day rather than later.

Thursday the 9th. Get started early on a home repair project. You will have more control over it if you take the reins now. Get a second opinion if it makes you more comfortable. An individual in your field will value your opinion. You may receive a job offer or moneymaking opportunity. To avoid risk, don't rush.

Friday the 10th. If you aren't sure where your priorities lie, you will waste precious energy. Be firm about where you will spend your time. An old friend may need your help. A family member may frustrate you with contradictory behavior. It will be in your best interest to get the matter clarified.

Saturday the 11th. You may be asking too much from a relative or housemate. Lowering your expectations will be a good idea if you don't have to compromise your values. A trip to the mall may find you something new for the home. Shop around for the best price on an expensive item. A family gathering will be relaxing.

Sunday the 12th. If you can, take care of responsibilities early in the day so you can play in the afternoon. Keep your worries to yourself, as a friend may be inclined to spread the word. Don't be tempted to reveal anything that may work against you later on. Try not to be too stubborn with loved ones.

Monday the 13th. You may be trying hard too hard within a romantic relationship. You will hear from a former love. Unfortunately one of you is not as interested as the other one is. You will be over it soon. This can be the day to have an important conversation with a child or teenager.

Tuesday the 14th. Start your day on a positive note. Give yourself a pep talk or do some affirmations. Recent events may have you feeling that you have lost the respect of a loved one but it's probably not true. In fact, you can be on the brink of some exciting changes. Tell someone how you feel and what you think. Be open.

Wednesday the 15th. This will be a mixed day. While things are likely to go very well for you on the job, financial worries may be upsetting. Things may not be under your control. You shouldn't let yourself get too upset over a situation you cannot change. An investment may require your attention now.

Thursday the 16th. Peace and harmony can be yours. Your charm can win the approval of a very important person. Those in sales or marketing will do well. All things having to do with self-improvement can be successful. An evening with that special someone can be the stuff that dreams are made of.

Friday the 17th. Your day will be filled with strange and lovely surprises. A phone call you receive will make you feel like a million bucks. Your generosity to a stranger will be repaid with joy. Matters of the heart are featured. People can be more loving than usual. The evening can bring you closer to those you love.

Saturday the 18th. Turn your attention to your health and well-being now. Destructive habits or self-indulgent behaviors can take their toll. Scale back on the things that aren't good for you and replace them with things that are. Serious matters like smoking may need medical advice.

Sunday the 19th. An optimistic attitude will work in your favor. If you are a single Capricorn, you may find that a happy-go-lucky style attracts the attention of an attractive stranger. A family member may approach you with an offer of financial backing.

Monday the 20th. Make your routine more fun. Try not to overstep your bounds on the job. Ask whether someone wants your help before stepping in and doing something you have not been asked to do. A financial decision you make with a partner can be very good. A far-off friend will appreciate a call.

Tuesday the 21st. Your way of thinking about serious things in life can land you in hot water if you share your thoughts. One of your co-workers may not agree with your spiritual or religious beliefs. If this is the case, keep your ideas to yourself. Avoid being overly critical of others, especially loved ones.

Wednesday the 22nd. An opportunity to broaden your horizons may come your way. It can be a smart move. Check out all of the details before you make any final decisions. An unexpected party invitation will make you feel lucky and loved. Start planning what to wear. A soothing late-night call will end an exciting day.

Thursday the 23rd. You may be quite ambitious now. Your energy level will be quite high, and you can even increase it with exercise early in the day. Outdoor and team sports are featured and you can excel in competitions. Teachers and legal professionals will be most helpful if you allow them to be.

Friday the 24th. Suspicions are aroused on the job. You may think someone is after your position. You may be right, but taking overt action will not be the best way to handle it. Improving your own job performance can get you noticed by the right people. You may even be offered a better job by a competitive firm.

Saturday the 25th. Be flexible; your plans may be changing more quickly than you expect. Exciting things may be coming your way. You can participate in a thrilling sport. Or perhaps your idea of excitement is playing a good word or number game. Enjoy.

Sunday the 26th. Try to spend some time with your friends if you can. The focus is on your hopes and wishes for the future. A good talk with an old pal may be just what the doctor ordered. Make sure the people you are with are supportive and helpful. Negative folks can really bring you down.

Monday the 27th. Even the best laid plans have to be changed sometimes, and this may be one of those days. You will be much happier with the new agenda if it provides an opportunity you would have otherwise missed. You may be feeling restless early in the day, but that should ease when you get some good news.

Tuesday the 28th. You may feel like staying in bed all day, and why not? If you can get away with it, take some time out to rest. Someone is looking to you for validation. You will be feeling upbeat this evening. Rather than entertain at home, go out to dinner if you can. Try someplace new. Relax and enjoy a change.

Wednesday the 29th. Take care of unfinished business before proceeding to fun things. A certain individual may be difficult to reach. This will be a good day to confront someone who has not been completely truthful with you. Keep your cool with loved ones. You have a lesson to learn from an older man.

Thursday the 30th. Appreciation for a job well done can be a welcome boost to your ego. You will enjoy an audience. Give special attention to deadlines, as you may be falling behind. You may be feeling distant from a loved one. A simple phone call can remedy the situation. If you are feeling overwhelmed, take a break.

Friday the 31st. You may have a lot to accomplish, but if you do it at a leisurely pace you probably will feel much better. A phone call from a business associate may bring good news involving your job status. Children and pets make you smile. Show your love.

Saturday September 1st. If you are feeling a little restless, buy something that will take your mind off other things. Perhaps your frustration with not being able to get out of the same old rut is wearing on you. Or you have been bogged down by studies. Allow yourself to enjoy wasting time without guilt.

Sunday the 2nd. You churchgoers may be tempted to skip the usual Sunday morning routine and sleep in. However, guilt is likely to get the better of you. Despite your tiredness, the sermon can be quite inspiring. You will be glad you pushed yourself out.

Monday the 3rd. If you are at work in a responsible position this Labor Day, try using honey rather than vinegar when it comes to confrontations. Staff, clients, and loved ones will follow your requests more readily if you treat them gently. Your significant other may be in a soft and romantic mood. You will be treated.

Tuesday the 4th. Now is the time for decisive action. You will not want to waste time with idle chitchat. Your roommates or loved ones are likely to pick up on any aggression and give you the room you need. Don't hesitate to tell them, however. When you work out at the gym, know your reasonable limits.

Wednesday the 5th. Inventory control may help you to streamline to avoid the unnecessary. Break free of extra social commitments this evening. You probably are in a mood to exert yourself lifting weights at the gym. Or perhaps a creative urge makes you want to redecorate the apartment. You will be frustrated if you set aside your priorities for friends and family.

Thursday the 6th. Impatient or speeding drivers may put you in an unpleasant mood as this day starts if you let them. However, once you spend a little time in peace, you can easily shake it off. Finish paperwork or errands. Cook your specialty for dinner tonight.

Friday the 7th. A pleasant day awaits you. A slow pace will suit you just fine. Your evening companion is likely to notice the extra care you have taken to dress nicely. A first date can be the start of a lovely long-term relationship. Consideration of a stranger's feelings will make an impression.

Saturday the 8th. An unhurried mood will continue. You may be delighted to check out garage sales or antique shops. Window-shopping with a loved one can be a pleasant way to spend a lazy day. Enjoy simple pleasures at your favorite place.

Sunday the 9th. If you're about to start a new school semester or job retraining, you may be preoccupied with getting yourself ready. Friends can keep you busy on the phone. You probably have a lot of little things to take care of. Stock up at the stationery store.

Monday the 10th. Those of you who are returning to school will find it delightful to see old friends and meet new ones. It can be easier than you expect to get into the routine. You Capricorn teachers will be in a very tolerant mood. Most of you will not get too much serious work done in this regard.

Tuesday the 11th. Teamwork can be the way to go. You will find the paperwork much more pleasant when you have another to exchange ideas with. If you need to make decisions about your schedule, you may find that you have more than one good option. Stay flexible and keep as much going as you can. What you learn will be to your advantage later.

Wednesday the 12th. Today's disruptions can slow you down, but your take-it-in-stride attitude will be helpful. If the computer is acting up, you should to take it in for repair as soon as possible to prevent larger problems. This can also be a good time for a car tune-up. Prevention can save you later headaches.

Thursday the 13th. A younger person, perhaps a child, may need quality attention. Such people can be a little shy about asking for help or talking about emotions. A little gift from you can allay their anxieties. Swimming can be a good way to end the day's tensions.

Friday the 14th. Your piggy bank may be holding more money than you realize. It may be time to roll up the coins and take a trip to the bank. Devise a plan to start saving a little more than you have been lately. The savings can be put toward that special vacation you are dreaming about, or your favorite charities.

Saturday the 15th. You may be in a take-charge mood. Since you have all the confidence in the world, why not make your big pitch to that incredible person to whom you are irresistibly attracted? You will be very successful in all you do. Go for the maximum. Self-promotion gets you noticed by the right person.

Sunday the 16th. This can be a good day to write some thank-you notes or letters you need to send. A little garden cleanup and weeding can be very therapeutic. You will be pleased with yourself if you follow through on attending a workshop or lecture. You will gain valuable information that can boost your personal effectiveness.

Monday the 17th. If you haven't been paying close attention to your diet, the scale may register higher than you expect. Don't be too upset. Perhaps your partner or roommate will diet with you. You may be too preoccupied to listen to someone's sob story.

Tuesday the 18th. New situations will be easier to handle. You may surprise yourself when you are the one to make the first move in a social setting. Or perhaps you are advocating new policies at the staff meeting, policies that you previously didn't want to accept. You can experiment with your style. Some Capricorns will be invited out to a special event.

Wednesday the 19th. Good ideas for making money can be popping into your head at a rapid pace. Follow your intuition. If you experiment with your sales approach, you will find your pitch more successful. Coincidence will be on your side. You may be in the right place at the right time.

Thursday the 20th. You may not be happy when friends cancel out. It may annoy you that they haven't given you enough time to rearrange your own schedule. However, an unexpected invitation from an older friend may fill your vacancy quite nicely.

Friday the 21st. It may be difficult to keep secrets to yourself; but if you are worried about competition, take extra care in casual conversations. Colleagues are probably more perceptive than you think at reading the thoughts behind your words. Don't fret about goals that may be out of reach. Be realistic with financial speculation.

Saturday the 22nd. You may have obligated yourself to more responsibilities than you can handle. You may not be happy about driving your children and the neighbors' children around. Make sure the other parents reciprocate. A toothache may warn you that you're overdue for a visit to the dentist.

Sunday the 23rd. A long-distance phone call from a parent or older relative can be quite pleasant. You may discuss an upcoming visit. A family get-together can go particularly smoothly. If the weather is good, a picnic will be very pleasant. Invite the neighbors too.

Monday the 24th. You can have an easy time justifying spending money on books or business travel. Technical manuals can be expensive, but it will be money well spent. Business travel will help to solve contractual problems or negotiations. All legal matters can be easily agreed upon; just know the facts.

Tuesday the 25th. This can be a push-pull day with fellow students or co-workers. You may register a little jealousy. If you can put aside what you are sensing, you will be able to prevent the start of an unpleasant relationship. Try to be as casual and friendly as possible, and you will turn a negative into a positive.

Wednesday the 26th. While you are so busy taking care of little details, you may miss important pieces of technical information. Don't be quick to accept advice at face value from an adviser or legal counselor. They may not have all the facts themselves. Shortsightedness can be problematic.

Thursday the 27th. Tell an irritating friend not to bother you any longer with whining and complaining. It will be easier than you think to divorce yourself from problems that really don't belong to you. It is time someone else made an equal contribution.

Friday the 28th. Spontaneous purchases can delight you. You may be on the market for a new car. A friend may find you the right vehicle or car dealership. Follow your intuition and don't hesitate to make a deal if it feels right. Celebrate with new music to listen to while driving. A party tonight may be scandalous.

Saturday the 29th. You will be an old softy. Romance may be in the air. You may plan a romantic candlelit evening with roses to grace the table. A sentimental movie can have you crying buckets, even if you have seen it previously and have the dialogue memorized. Sleep well, and you will have pleasant dreams.

Sunday the 30th. An older friend who feels quite paternal toward you may bring you a treat or a good piece of advice. Exchanging recipes or stories can take up a large portion of your visit together. You may be helpful in recommending vitamins or good doctors. A small mechanical problem can be easily fixed.

Monday October 1st. Those of you who are married should make a special date with your spouse for this evening. The romance level can be too high to record. If you're not married but thinking of asking someone for a date, tonight's the night. Don't be shy.

Tuesday the 2nd. Your curiosity will get the best of you if you don't control your impulses. You will not be welcome in other people's business. Wait until you have all the facts. Try to be more attentive to those you love. A compromise may not be in your nature, but it can help anyway.

Wednesday the 3rd. Patience with a sibling may be called for. Be careful with numbers. You can avoid an error by double-checking math and counting money twice. You may be torn between work and fun. A little of both will be the best. Finish your work early then party. These can be dreamy times.

Thursday the 4th. If you have been avoiding a sibling, this can be a good time to make contact. Giving someone the silent treatment will not work. Pay close attention to safety rules now, especially in dangerous activities and sports. A potential accident will be just a near miss thanks to your quick thinking.

Friday the 5th. Something that happened in your family history will be of interest to you now. Grandparents may be more than willing to share some fascinating tidbits. You will want to write some of these stories down for future generations to enjoy. A child can benefit from your undivided attention.

Saturday the 6th. A family member may be exaggerating or overoptimistic. Show gratitude to your spouse and kids. You may want to cook them a festive dinner. Sparks may ignite between couples and you can find yourself in a romantic situation sooner than you imagined. Solitude can be blissful as well.

Sunday the 7th. Expect confirmation from an unexpected source. Someone you admire will share the sentiment. Watch the behavior of a child closely. It may be more important than you think. Participating in sports or physical activities with your family members can be a healthy way of becoming closer.

Monday the 8th. Responsibilities must come before pleasure. If you take care of your work first, you can have more fun with less guilt. Your boss will be impressed if you complete your work on time. You can be tempted to make big travel plans but you may save money if you wait a day or two.

Tuesday the 9th. Speak slowly and clearly. Anything that seems confused should be clarified immediately. Pay attention to details, especially to numbers. A mathematical error is possible. Don't believe everything you hear. Reality is relative according to point of view.

Wednesday the 10th. Sincere flattery is always welcome. You may consider giving a gift to someone who has been helpful. Actions like these can work in your favor, as folks love it at this time. Your spouse or lover may be overdue for a little pampering this evening.

Thursday the 11th. Relationships may be tense all around. A certain someone probably just wants more attention. People at work may be proud, arrogant, and wound up in their own problems. Try not to give advice. By the weekend, folks will be much more fun and open. A surprise can be in the cards.

Friday the 12th. You may want to take a mental health day at home even if you're scheduled to work. Solitude brings a certain feeling that nothing else can match. Spend the day quietly reading a book, looking through old photos, or planning a surprise for your significant other. You will be relieved if a long-standing project comes to a conclusion now.

Saturday the 13th. Fix broken things around the house before they get out of hand and grate on your nerves. Let out physical energy in positive ways such as bicycling, walking, running, and team sports.

Sunday the 14th. Try not to take on more than you can handle, especially when it comes to physical work. A relative's request may seem a bit odd. Think twice if that's the case. A miscommunication with a family member can cause a temporary rift. You will be able to smooth it over if your intentions are sincere.

Monday the 15th. Those of you who are students will need to study a little harder. You may not be prepared for an upcoming exam. Travel is featured, so be spontaneous if you can. Pack extra clothing in case you decide to stay longer.

Tuesday the 16th. Now's the time to clear up a misunderstanding. Follow through on unfinished business so you can move ahead in your work. Words can take on greater importance. You may want to write a paper or article. Mix business with pleasure.

Wednesday the 17th. A gift may be coming your way. You may take a trip with your winnings. Your tact will save the day. Don't let an insensitive person get the best of you. Watch the pennies; you have a tendency to overspend. Keep a negative comment to yourself.

Thursday the 18th. You can come across an interesting idea through a conversation with an older person. Pay attention; this one can be worth remembering. Make a plan and act quickly. Follow your heart in romance. You may be in the running for a promotion.

Friday the 19th. A co-worker looks up to you as a role model. Your integrity will set a positive example. A labor dispute can result in a pay raise, but don't expect it to happen overnight. Helping a rebellious teenager will be a labor of love. Stay home tonight if possible.

Saturday the 20th. A good friend may need your compassion right now. Just listening may be the best thing to do. Unsolicited advice may not be welcome. A sense of humor is the best weapon against boredom. If you're feeling angry or frustrated, punching a pillow can be a great relief. Talk with a trusted friend about a dream job you have been considering.

Sunday the 21st. Decipher your dreams. You may be having some wild ones these days. Don't rely on a dream book in order to understand the symbolism. What does your intuition tell you? Take some time out to do whatever it is that feeds your soul. Although someone may try to push your buttons, suspend judgment. You never know what motivates people.

Monday the 22nd. People can be demanding of your time right now. You will feel less pressured if you can find out which tasks are most important and concentrate on those. You can accomplish a great deal if you are focused, and you have chance for victory.

Tuesday the 23rd. Projects that have been on hold can be jump-started; let the momentum grow. It is an important day for getting in touch with higher-ups. A supervisor will be on your side. Negotiations can reach agreement. Do not overestimate your abilities.

Wednesday the 24th. Someone you meet will make a significant impact on your outlook. You may want to do a reality check on your appearance. Self-image can be everything, and your look should match the impression you want to give. A disagreement with a young man is possible if you aren't flexible.

Thursday the 25th. Restlessness can get you into hot water. You probably will want to do something outside of your routine. If you're thinking of making a radical change in your appearance, think again. This may not be the best time to get a tattoo or to dye your hair.

Friday the 26th. Moneymaking opportunities can abound for those of you who are looking. You may earn a few bucks by selling something you no longer want. Holding a yard or garage sale or getting a table at a flea market can be a way for you to meet more neighbors too. Hold your tongue if you start to criticize a loved one. A gentle approach will work best.

Saturday the 27th. A situation involving your spouse and family members may require you to act as a mediator. Romance can be tricky. You may be attracted to the wrong person. Take a good look if you think this is possible.

Sunday the 28th. People at home may be missing you like crazy, especially if you have been away or working long hours. Spending unnecessary time away can upset them. If you absolutely cannot be with your loved ones, you should try to make up for it later.

Monday the 29th. A neighborhood or community celebration will be a wonderful way to spend the day. Children may want to get involved, and they can be most helpful. Your family will be foremost in your mind at this time. You may have to make a financial decision before the day's end. Go with your heart; then rest assured that you have made the best possible choice.

Tuesday the 30th. Money worries may be a blessing in disguise. An honest examination of what is really going on can lead to a breakthrough in how you handle your money. Overspending has got to stop. Someone you meet can literally change your life. Be open to the possibilities. It's okay to be impulsive in love.

Wednesday the 31st. Use care with documents. It is possible to make a mistake. Don't sign a paper if you don't understand or aren't comfortable with it. Taking a risk will not be wise. Take things slow and easy; you will get what you want in the end.

Thursday November 1st. People will be more cooperative than usual. Sales and marketing projects will go better than expected. Share the wealth by hiring others to do the jobs you no longer want to do. Focus on the things you like and how you can make your ideas and projects pay off. Put a few dollars aside to use for a special treat in the near future.

Friday the 2nd. It can be a lot of fun, recalling old times. You may be asked to participate in a group project. This may lead to bigger and better things, so give it thought. Put your talents to use in a creative endeavor. Don't hesitate to ask for help if you need it.

Saturday the 3rd. Travel may be on the agenda. Kids will be pleasant and fun. Playing games can be fun for the whole family. You may find it easier than usual to talk to new people. This will work in your favor when it comes to love and romance.

Sunday the 4th. Health and friendship are featured. Get together with friends for some fun exercise. Hiking, biking, and walking can be good ways to enjoy fresh air and get your blood pumping. Try to eat nutritious food, as greasy or too sweet things can have a negative effect on your body. If you're trying to break a habit, a friend may be able to help.

Monday the 5th. Make a list of priority jobs, and stick to it. Take care of your least favorite duties first to prevent procrastination. Give yourself a deadline if you really feel like avoiding a job. Daydreaming can lead to an excellent moneymaking idea. Write your thoughts down so you don't forget them.

Tuesday the 6th. When is the last time you did something special for yourself? Take some time out of a busy schedule just for you. Shopping will yield good deals. You may find some wonderful new clothing that makes you feel like a million bucks.

Wednesday the 7th. A significant relationship that has been through some rocky times can be on your mind. You may be able to do a lot toward repairing any damage that has been done. Putting your partner's feelings before your own may be necessary. A sense of humor helps too. Be optimistic about a business deal.

Thursday the 8th. Important issues with loved ones may need to be considered. Your thoughtfulness and respect can make a potentially difficult situation easier. Business partnerships can use a little attention. Don't speak for another if you can possibly avoid it.

Friday the 9th. Spending money that's not yours can get you into trouble. Leave the credit cards at home if you think you shouldn't use them. Don't make decisions about a joint bank account without consulting the other party. A friend may be causing you some concern. It will be best to avoid him or her for a few days or even longer until the trouble blows over.

Saturday the 10th. Talk openly with a family member with whom you disagree. We all are entitled to our own opinions, and sometimes there is no right or wrong. Take a few minutes to allay a loved one's anxiety. Expect the unexpected when it comes to travel. Allow time for changes along the way.

Sunday the 11th. Research can reveal some interesting and perhaps even disturbing news. Friends and family alike may be ultrasensitive. You can avoid a misunderstanding if you are thoughtful. Minor scuffles have a way of getting bigger. Be considerate.

Monday the 12th. Your plans for romance may not be as simple as you think. The person you have in mind can have other ideas. Work may interfere with your plans for play. No expectations, no disappointments can be a good motto. A plan for a trip or vacation may need a few adjustments. Be flexible if you can.

Tuesday the 13th. You may feel like you're stuck in a groove. Making minor changes can help to put an end to boredom. Perhaps you can rearrange your work space or add some interesting art. Getting better organized can put an end to time-consuming chores.

Wednesday the 14th. Your philosophies about life may come to the forefront as you meet someone new, possibly on the job. You can talk to this person easily. A magnetic attraction to a stranger can lead to romance if you let it. If you expect to be dealing with a legal matter, make sure you're prepared.

Thursday the 15th. You may be feeling extra confident. Luck will be with you. If you turn on the charm when dealing with others, you will win their affection. Pay attention to your highest ambitions. What is one thing you can do to reach your goals? Even the smallest steps can count. Go ahead and ask for a favor.

Friday the 16th. Getting along with people may be harder than usual. A power struggle can take place or you may clash with a friend. You may resent someone who holds authority over you. If backed into a corner, you may say something you will regret later. Try to think before you speak. It's okay to confront someone, but not impulsively or in anger.

Saturday the 17th. If you can, escape in some way. Reading a good book, maybe an adventure novel, can be excellent. If you're traveling, notice the cultural differences between where you are and where you live. Go with your instincts this evening.

Sunday the 18th. It may seem that benevolent forces are working to assist you. People will be friendly and helpful. Great ideas can be coming to you. The future looks wide open. Spend some time meditating or reflecting on your life. Try not to be compulsive about your ambitions at this time.

Monday the 19th. Daydreaming can delay getting the job done. If you can avoid it, you will get more accomplished at work. You may be feeling quite ambitious. You will have more personal magnetism and power. Business appointments can go well.

Tuesday the 20th. Your job will be frustrating if you are impatient. Dramatic encounters with people at work must be avoided like the plague. Stay on the sidelines when it comes to other people's arguments. If you get involved, you may live to regret it. Turn a deaf ear to office gossip, which may turn malicious.

Wednesday the 21st. Your special abilities come into focus, and you will be recognized for your talent. A hobby or creative endeavor will give you pleasure. Be practical and flexible when it comes to making a financial decision. Taking a gamble is not necessarily a good thing at this time. Speak slowly and carefully when giving directions lest they be heard incorrectly.

Thursday the 22nd. This Thanksgiving Day you may not agree with a significant other when it comes to money. Wait to sign on a major purchase such as real estate or a car. Take time to gather all the facts. Holiday dinner guests can give you some good suggestions. Domestic affairs may offer a challenge. Stand your ground firmly without being aggressive.

Friday the 23rd. A quiet time with loved ones can be special. Solitude is your next best bet. Don't feel guilty if you don't want to get out of your pajamas all day. You deserve a break. If you must work, a smile can make the day brighter for everyone. A candlelit dinner with wine and roses can advance romance.

Saturday the 24th. Money can be a concern if a project is too expensive. You're resourceful so you can find a way around it. Someone close to you may have the answer. A check you have been expecting may be delayed but it will be only for a short while. Do all that you can and let time do the rest.

Sunday the 25th. You can suddenly find a new friend or even romance through local activities. Community and neighborhood projects may be on the agenda. Your talents and abilities can be very valuable to a nonprofit organization. Service your car and other machinery to be sure that everything is safe and ready for action.

Monday the 26th. Cooperation can get you what you need. Be open to suggestions. People are bright and resourceful now. Delegate minor responsibilities. You probably should be running your own show, however, and one person may have to be told so.

Tuesday the 27th. Transportation may not be reliable. Leave early for an important appointment since traffic can be heavy or another surprise can occur. You will impress someone important by being enthusiastic and motivated. Competitive sports and games can do the trick if you're feeling aggressive.

Wednesday the 28th. Domestic concerns can affect your work performance if you're not careful. Take care of little jobs around the house when you can so they don't pile up. A phone call or letter to a distant relative will be a nice gesture. An influential family member can be helpful to you if you ask. You may have to let go of a stubborn point of view.

Thursday the 29th. You may be ultrasensitive, which can make you feel uncomfortable in social situations. Staying at home may be the solution to this very temporary problem. Treat yourself to some of the physical comforts of life such as a good dinner.

Friday the 30th. Simple changes made in and around your home can make a big difference in the way you feel. Introduce wind chimes or a whimsical garden accessory. Take a few minutes this evening to put your feet up. Those of you who meditate will find it especially helpful now.

Saturday December 1st. Art and music bring joy. Your creative talents can lead to a moneymaking opportunity. Children may be helpful. Don't be surprised if a friendship heats up without warning. You romantics will make the most of a magical evening.

Sunday the 2nd. If you're dragging your heels about a fitness program, go with a friend. Working out together will be a great idea, especially if you are busy and have little time for friends. Getting out into nature can be soothing and inspiring as well as good exercise.

Monday the 3rd. A new romantic situation can be misleading. You are very idealistic right now. Perhaps you are seeing stars when it comes to an attractive person. A project can become a little tricky if you try to cut corners. Try to get some rest and relaxation.

Tuesday the 4th. Rise to any challenges presented to you, as you will be energetic and motivated. You can be quite assertive and ready to tackle an obstacle over which you may have been procrastinating. Recognize an opportunity in romance and make the most of it.

Wednesday the 5th. You may feel that everything is against you, but that is not so. A partnership can seem like an obstacle if you don't get what you want. You probably are being challenged to take care of business on a more responsible level.

Thursday the 6th. Any difficulties within a significant relationship will be overcome, especially if you are giving it your all. Don't expect to be completely out of the water for a while yet, but good progress is likely. If you're feeling low, count your blessings.

Friday the 7th. You can make a really good decision on joint finances. You may want to go partying or hang around with friends tonight. Take care of your responsibilities first. People can be critical, so don't take it personally. Use tact if you must criticize another.

Saturday the 8th. You may get a chance to do some partying and make new contacts. Don't turn down any social invitations or choose only the ones with the most opportunity to meet interesting people. Keep the magic in your relationship alive. A romantic opportunity may be in the cards.

Sunday the 9th. Research projects can be promising. The time you spend will be well rewarded. Your efforts toward helping a partner will be noticed and acknowledged. Do it without expecting anything in return. Delegate responsibilities to a younger person who wants to help. A friend will confide in you. He or she may not be asking for advice, just for a sympathetic ear.

Monday the 10th. Issues within a relationship can reach the breaking point. Your ability to resolve the problem will be excellent; the solutions you come up with may surprise even yourself. Take responsibility for your actions and commit to making it work.

Tuesday the 11th. You may feel that you're ready for a career change. If so, keep your eyes and ears open for clues. Mention it to friends and acquaintances. Traveling long distance can broaden your horizons and provide inspiration for the future. Travel plans may come up with little or no notice.

Wednesday the 12th. Competition is tough. You want to be the best in your field. Know who your competitors are. You may need to update your skills or presentation. Imitation is the sincerest form of flattery and a good way to get career direction. Gather knowledge and inspiration from someone you admire.

Thursday the 13th. Folks at work can be helpful and pleasant. This will be a better time than usual to ask for a special favor. You can delegate responsibilities in order to lighten your load. This will free you to work on projects to which you are more suited.

Friday the 14th. Projects to start now include new savings accounts, businesses, or anything that requires signing a contract. Romantic relationships heat up. Get away with the one you love. At the very least, plan a date for this evening.

Saturday the 15th. A project will run much more smoothly if you have taken care of all the details. If you have any questions at all, just follow your hunch. Even when something does go amiss, your quick response can save the day. You may be kept waiting for an appointment. Escape into a good book.

Sunday the 16th. Try to get out and have some real fun. Take a child to see Christmas lights or a special event. Let yourself be zany and kooky. Kicking around the neighborhood with a friend can be a blast. Even shopping can be fun if you have the right attitude.

Monday the 17th. Folks may not be too reliable. If a job really needs doing, do it yourself. A trip may be interrupted by responsibilities at home. You can be in for a big surprise at work. Changes in management may be in effect. Keep on your toes if you think your performance is coming up for review.

Tuesday the 18th. Your net worth can be increased through changes you implement now. Market yourself or your product. You may sell something you want to get rid of, such as a car or piece of equipment. Watch yourself with relationships, however, as your luck is not likely to extend into that area of your life. Someone eccentric has a message for you.

Wednesday the 19th. Pay close attention to detail. Little things have a way of getting out of hand. Try to avoid confusion by communicating in a very clear manner, especially with written, faxed, or e-mailed documents. Take a co-worker's story with a grain of salt. Try to be honest when telling your own stories.

Thursday the 20th. If you have paperwork piling up, clear it out. If you wait much longer, it will be unmanageable. Return phone calls and take care of other minor details. This can be an enchanted evening. People will be friendly and open.

Friday the 21st. Your positive attitude can take you far. Try not to be disappointed if things don't go exactly as planned. There are other days; you can lay the groundwork now to get results later. Your instincts will point you in the right direction. Trust them.

Saturday the 22nd. Misunderstandings can and should be cleared up immediately. Take care of unfinished business, as procrastinating can put you under pressure later on. Double-check all spelling and mathematics. Allow yourself to be creative. If you do art of any kind, make it a point to do so now.

Sunday the 23rd. You may find a new friend or even a romance through local activities. Community and neighborhood projects will be on the agenda. Your talents and abilities can be very valuable to a nonprofit organization. Be prepared if you're traveling for the holidays. Get out and join the festivities.

Monday the 24th. You will be giving selfless service now, whether working in a soup kitchen, passing out treats at a local hospital, or working directly in your own neighborhood. If you are unable to give of yourself in this manner, think about what you can do. Perhaps you have a family member who is in need of help, or a friend is feeling low. You can make a difference.

Tuesday the 25th. Merry Christmas! You Capricorns aren't always demonstrative, so you may be surprised when you become a bit misty at times this holiday. Family traditions will be more meaningful than modern versions. You may be more talkative than usual. Don't be afraid to express your love and gratitude.

Wednesday the 26th. Family ties can be strengthened. Spending time at home with children can bring great satisfaction. Neighborhood activities such as sports and local theater presentations can be enjoyed by all. This is not an exciting time, but a heartwarming and relaxing one. Try to get some solitude at some point.

Thursday the 27th. You may be physically tired. Quality family time will be the best now and can include indoor sports such as swimming or skating. You will not be disappointed by your children. Reward them for good behavior. Romantic times continue, and new partnerships can grow by leaps and bounds.

Friday the 28th. Young people can be creative, mischievous, and fun. Being around them will bring back your own childhood and the innocence of youth. Working on projects that express your special talents can recharge your batteries. A neighbor will be thankful if you volunteer your help on a project.

Saturday the 29th. The best way to spend the day can be just to stay home and do maintenance chores. You may be feeling wiped out from all of the excitement of the past week. Try to be completely alone. Meditation, reflection, and prayer are very helpful.

Sunday the 30th. If the stress of the holiday season is getting to you, try to take some time to pamper yourself. Career concerns can be placed on the back burner for a few more days. Whatever is happening, do your best and leave it at that. As long as you know in your heart that you have done a good job, just let it go.

Monday the 31st. You will not want to stay home tonight. You will be feeling exuberant, optimistic, and happy. In the early part of the day, you may be a little withdrawn, but by evening you will be outgoing again. There may be one person in particular who ruffles your feathers, but try to forget about it for tonight.

Advertisement

Advertisement

Advertisement

Advertisement